WOMEN LEADING IN OUR NEW WORLD

Edited by
Jo Baldwin

PROPER BOOKS

WOMEN LEADING IN OUR NEW WORLD

Edited by
Jo Baldwin

In support of Soul Sisters Empowering People UK
PROPER BOOKS

DISCLAIMER

Women Leading In Our New World is intended for information and education purposes only. This book does not constitute specific legal, financial, clinical or commercial advice unique to your situation.

The views and opinions expressed in this book are those of the authors and do not reflect those of the Publisher and Resellers, who accept no responsibility for loss, damage or injury to persons or their belongings as a direct or indirect result of reading this book.

All people mentioned in case studies have been used with permission, and/or have had names, genders, industries and personal details altered to protect client confidentiality. Any resemblance to persons living or dead is purely coincidental.

A CIP catalogue record for this book is available from the British Library.

Published by Proper Books
properbookspublishing@gmail.com

- -

CONTENTS

By Sarah Presley

By Caroline Durham

By Tracey Miller

By Teresa Corso

By Gill McKay

By Rosanna Hanness

By Adelle Helen Martin

By Gigi Brown

By Jo Baldwin

FOREWORD
VALUES, WHERE IT ALL STARTS
By Asma Begum

I am excited and thrilled to be offering you, the reader of this incredible book, its first words.

Hi! I'm Asma, founder of a charity whose values are inclusion, trust, respect, empowerment and compassion. We are called Soul Sisters: Empowering People.

I founded Soul Sisters in Rochdale in January 2020, and my intention was to make sure that the charity is available to everyone and anyone who's been affected by domestic abuse. That could be women, men and children. And not just the victim, but also their family members, friends, work colleagues, professionals. We are widely open to everyone because we want to raise awareness collectively, about domestic abuse.

I'd like to share with you the five values of Soul Sisters as these have not only led us to be where we are today, but have also led many women onto a different path where once they saw no options, including me.

The first Soul Sisters value of compassion goes deep, and is interlinked with the other values. When someone has gone through abuse, the last thing they need is someone not to listen to them, not to believe them, to start judging them and telling them what to do.

Compassion means that we care about that person, we're giving them that space, and respecting them for their story, and we don't want to change that story. What we want to do is help them grow away and move forward from that painful situation, to have that listening ear validating what the person is seeing, being kind to them and letting them find the solutions.

Empowerment is, on its own, a very big thing. It means giving that person or any of the service users the space to find their lives again, find themselves again and move forward. One of our service users came to us last year and with the help of our charity she is now one of our volunteers and actually holds one of the main positions within the charity. That is only because her confidence and self esteem increased. She has been empowered to move on. Through our services she started to understand the reasons for how she was feeling. She started to understand what happened to her, to clarify what was abuse and what wasn't. Through our awareness sessions she has been empowered to find information and learn and make different choices.

Setting up a charity was not something that I actually thought about before, I never planned for it. But I always knew that there was something I wanted to do to help other people that have gone through adversity, but I never knew how, until I went through it myself. I went through the journey of getting help and asking for help, professional help, I learned so much. I believe if I had not go through what I went through, I would not be able to run the charity as it is. I feel I've learned this so that I can share this knowledge with other people because they're going to be stuck like me. They're going to be crossing the road and crying when a solicitor is not listening to them, feeling hopelessly lost. This was my experience and I feel that I should share the knowledge and help as many people as I can.

One of the first ways I thought of sharing my knowledge was public speaking, so that's how I started, with truth. I was then offered more events, and the audience shared that they valued what I was saying. This really helped me build my confidence.

My next role was volunteering and in that space, I was given another insight into what could be done, and what I could do to raise awareness and help people to learn about domestic abuse. Just before the pandemic I was speaking at an event 'Womankind' in Preston and again, the amount of feedback I received was amazing even though I was really nervous. So many comments came back saying how well I was doing, that I was so passionate, and that my message needed to be shared and discussed.

When the pandemic hit, I started group sessions on WhatsApp and on Zoom, but I was sometimes working 24 hours a day. Sometimes I was not eating properly, but when I could see the potential of it becoming a charity I took on board trustees, and we created a charity, Soul Sisters.

One of the reasons I wanted to call it something else other than domestic abuse is that I didn't want to make it obvious. I wanted to make it something that sounds like it's connecting us. One of the things that we do at Soul Sisters is peer support. That means you're understanding each other's *lived* experience. You're guiding each other. You're sharing techniques with each other, on how to survive. It was really important to me that we had the right name and message from the outset.

Where am I now? I am in a much better place and I feel that if I didn't have the charity I would be struggling, maybe mentally unwell, especially over the pandemic, when everyone was talking about domestic abuse. It can be very triggering. There are lots of TV soaps covering domestic abuse in their storylines. It can be difficult. But the charity kept me alive and kept me sane as I gradually built my confidence and I found the old Asma again.

There was still a little voice in the background saying, 'You can't do this', and 'You're not going to be able to do this, it will fail', but because of support from the trustees and friends, I kept going.

I currently have a court case running, but I have flexibility to run the charity as much or as less as I want. We now have a number of volunteers and we are well known within the borough of Rochdale and are growing a global reach, too.

We have a number of service users coming from different backgrounds, different ages, and different genders, who, somehow or another, are hearing about the Soul Sisters.

As a reader of this collective message of truth and leadership, I invite you to join us, too, whether or not you have experienced domestic violence. Knowing more about it and how it can impact us, can empower you to have better conversations and perhaps be the compassionate solicitor, the listening sister or the kind friend who can sense things are very wrong.

Thank you to Jo for inviting me to write the introduction for this book, there are powerful and painful stories shared, but all will give you a defining sense of inspiration to lead more in our evolving world.

About Asma Begum

Asma is a British Bangladeshi mum living in North UK and is a survivor of domestic abuse.Using her own experiences to inspire and motivate other women also wishing to turn their lives around, Asma is proud to have  founded her own organisation, Soul Sisters: Empowering People, a Charitable Incorporated Organisation. The charity helps women, men and children overcome the negative impact on health, wellbeing and happiness caused by the trauma of domestic abuse.

She is a BA (Hons) Law & Sociology Graduate, a certified NLP and Timeline Soul Connecting Coach and Creative Engagement Assistant at Manchester International Festival (MIF).

She lives independently, raising her son, being a positive role model, good citizen and volunteer, social justice activist and is embarking on the journey of female entrepreneurship to support women in need.

Asma is on her writing path, planning her own book sharing her experience, and also exploring the power of poetry. She loves most to spend her time immersed in nature with her son. Connect with Asma at www.soulsisters.org.uk

'O WAI WAU?' WHO AM I?
By Kumu Brenda Mohalapua Ignacio

'O Wai Wau? (Who am I?) was my soulful question of childhood as I lay on my grandmother's lawn, gazing up at the vastness of the blue sky and puffy clouds of my birthplace, the beautiful island of Hawaii. 'Who am I?'

I was born in the territory of Hawaii shortly after the bombing of Pearl Harbor in December of 1941. My sense of peace and innate joy could not yet comprehend all that my life would present. Celebrations, obstacles, and other life lessons were yet to come. I now know that these were opportunities to build strength and to grow in consciousness.

My elders taught me that in order to learn I was to listen and observe. Often powerful teachings were in the form of stories and parables and one of the earliest examples, The Bowl of Light, is found in Pali Jae Lee's book 'Tales of the Night Rainbow'. This teaching is a key to understanding WHO I AM.

"Each child at birth has a bowl of perfect Light. If she tends her Light it will grow in strength and she can do all things. Swim with the shark, fly with the birds, know and understand all things. If, however, she becomes envious or jealous, she drops a stone into her Bowl of Light and some of the Light goes out. Light and the stone cannot hold the same space. If she continues to put stones into the Bowl of Light the Light will go out and she will become a stone. A stone does not grow, nor does it move. If at any time she tires of being a stone all she needs to do is turn the bowl upside down and the stones will fall away and the Light will grow once more."

My mother passed at a young age, and I was blessed to have Nana Veary as my mentor and 'spiritual mother.' Hannah 'Nana' Veary is known internationally for her wisdom and her sharing of her journey as a teacher and as a Hawaiian Elder. Her book, 'Change We Must' is a powerful and cherished gift.

With her I was given many extraordinary experiences, including a private audience with the Dalai Lama. Nana once said to me, rather forcefully, "Mohalapua, you have NO IDEA of ALL THAT YOU ARE!" I was stunned at her words, and my inner child asked, "Really?"

I had been raised to be ha'aha'a, or humble and modest, as well as olu'olu, which is agreeable, expressed with pleasantness. These traits are an important part of being Hawaiian and living with Aloha. Aloha identifies one readily in most, if not all, parts of the world. It is most often suggested to mean hello, goodbye and love but 'Aloha' has a far deeper meaning.

Pilahi Paki wrote the true meaning of Aloha, and it is our way of life, gives us power and keeps us in balance and harmony with life. Each letter of the word has its own meaning:

A - Akahai, meaning kindness, expressed with tenderness.
L – Lokahi, meaning unity, expressed with harmony.
O – Olu'olu, meaning agreeable, expressed with pleasantness.
H – Ha'aha'a, meaning humility, expressed with modesty.
A – Ahonui, meaning patience, expressed with perseverance.

These principles and kindness were my guiding spiritual foundation.

Where had my life not given me a true sense of 'O Wai Wau," or all that I was?

Hardships brought on by a war that was not a part of our way of life harshly impacted our families. Where kindness, trust, sharing and oneness of all ethnicities once existed, the war seemed extremely invasive.

For example, Japanese residents were unfairly sent to concentration camps, causing pain for many. Despite this, some of Hawaii's Japanese enlisted in the armed forces, were sent to Europe and outlying areas, and bravely served in the U.S. military.

Although very young, my innate joy was misunderstood after the war which had altered Hawaii's people's sense of happiness and trust. Life was hard. Thinking it was the correct thing to do, I receded into a quieter, thoughtful place so as not to annoy.

A life enhancing gift was when Nana used the traditional manner of bestowing my Hawaiian name on me after meditation, prayer and listening to ancestors. The meaning of it sounded far too lofty to me, and I questioned my worth. I do believe that as women, we are often led to question our worth, conditioned by societal dictates, no matter where in this world we find ourselves.

The Hawaiian name Nana was led to name me was Mohalapua which has the following empowering meaning:

Mohala – Unfolding, blossoming, shining forth as a light; appearing clear, as a thought; evolved; free from fear or worry.

Pua – Flower

In her wisdom, Nana intuited that my inner child was indeed born a Bowl of Light yet as my family and Hawaii had experienced the ravages and suffering of war stones had been placed into my Bowl. And not of my inner child's choosing.

Having this name and Nana's encouragement has led me to empowering others to know their worth and to bring forth healing within themselves.

Another 'stone' was placed in my Bowl in 1946, when a devastating tsunami destroyed a school and took many lives, including three of my young cousins. The grief enveloped our family, and as a four-year-old all I could feel was overwhelming sadness and confusion.   With Nana's guidance I learned how to release the stones and allow my Light to shine once more.

Women are gifted in so many ways and leadership is easily within our grasp. My greatest example is Hawaii's last reigning monarch, Queen Liliuokalani.

Queen Liliuokalani was illegally overthrown in 1893, and imprisoned in L'olani Palace, the only palace on American soil. Hawaii's annexation to the United States followed. Knowing that Hawaii could not withstand resisting the overthrow, she protected her people with great courage. While imprisoned, she wrote 'The Queen's Prayer', asking God to protect her people and to forgive those who led the overthrow. Our Queen was extremely intelligent, kind, powerful, and highly regarded by Great Britain. Mutual respect and friendship led to our flag resembling the British flag. She is one of my greatest inspirations.

It is my strong belief that the current world climate calls for women to be leaders. The needs of Mother Nature as well as the healing of divisions underscores this truth. We, as women, can help to restore our world to peaceful renewal and vibrancy. It is more than time that we reclaim our worth and gifts, going forth mindfully, tending to our inner fire with a sense of renewed light, warmth, and inspired creation. Our souls seek fulfilment! We do not need permission to be all that we can be.

Hawaii offers encouragement to do this. There is our word MANA, a word of *beingness*. It is a healing life force that permeates the universe, an intentional source of power. How do we get *mana*?

We learn to listen to our inner voice and invite divine intuition. We practice physical balance, with exercise and rest, and spend time in nature, which radiates *mana*. We practice forgiveness, go with the flow, and let go of the past. We seek knowledge, learn new things, and focus our hearts on Trust. And one last thing, we get *mana* by assuring our inner child that we love her and will always take care of her and let her out to play.

Hawaii also has the word PONO. Being *pono* contributes to inner harmony. It is always doing what is right and always telling the truth. Also, it is letting go of drama in our lives. It is knowing our worth, that we are love and that we are loved. Forgiving ourselves if we have "missed the mark" and forgiving others thereby cleaning our slates and choosing instead to reclaim our truth.

An important traditional practice, known as *ho'oponopono* means 'to make things right'. My elders entrusted me with this practice and I became a practitioner of reestablishing 'lokahi', or 'unity' for individuals, families, institutions and businesses. When we have unity we are in balance and have spiritual power. We, as women, often have the intuition and an innate ability to love unconditionally as well as the wisdom to solve problems.

I joyously share our 'Mission Statement' in Hawaii, which says "Care for the air, care for the water, care for our spirit, for self and others, and how we treat one another." This statement brings unity and power to come forth. I restate my heartfelt belief that we, as women, can come forth and become leaders, as our guidance is assuredly needed. If we go forth and encourage change in our global discouragement for leadership by women, the earth will become heaven. Our strength comes from our disallowing comparisons, working together with compassion and our loving hearts. Let us release our outdated fears brought on by the noise of ego and perceived separation and go forth.

In Hawaii, this is called IMUA, or "Going forth with strength." Time for change without fear. 'O wau 'o Mohalapua! I AM Mohalapua! 'O wai' oe? Who are YOU? 'O wai makou? Who are WE?

Please know that I hold each of you with unconditional love and give you permission to use the definition of my Hawaiian name and soul essence as a goal, as in giving yourself encouragement to blossom forth, shine your light, enhance your clear thoughts, and become free of fear or worry.

Pomaika'i Na Mea Apau! "Everything is blessed!"

15

About Kumu Lomilomi Brenda Mohalapua Ignacio, LMT, CLP

Brenda Mohalapua Ignacio is a Kumu Lomilomi and DOE Licensed Instructor of Hawaiian Healing Arts. She has appeared in several films on Hawaiian Healing, shown on several islands as part of the  International Film Festivals, including "Hawaiian Healing," "Hawaiian Meditations" and "Pule Wailele," for which, as coordinating producer, she shared in winning a coveted Telly Award in 2007. She has also been featured in magazines and books on Lomilomi Massage, including "Hawaiian Massage, Lomilomi ~ Sacred Touch of Aloha."

Co-founder of Hawaii Healing Arts College in Kailua, Oahu, Kumu Brenda loves to teach students the wisdom given to her by her own teachers, many of whom entrusted her with formerly secret knowledge. Credentials include Licensed Massage Therapist, Hawaii Licensed Kahu, Hawaii DOE Licensed Instructor, NCBTMB Provider A for CE credits, and Former Director and Approved Instructor with the Hawaiian Lomilomi Association.

She has traveled extensively throughout the U.S., Europe and Asia as part of her Island heritage, representing the State of Hawaii and speaking on cultural richness and oneness. She, together with Spiritual Teacher Nana Veary, author of "Change We Must," met privately with the Dalai Lama in Hawaii during the 1980s. As a student of Nana's since 1975, she considers Nana to be one of the main sources of her passion for lomilomi and ho'oponopono, and Nana's spirit infuses her classes. A native of Hamakua, Big Island of Hawaii, Kumu Brenda was taught from birth the connection of the spirit of love in all things, especially nature, by her grandmother Mary Silva. Hawaii's Queen Lili'uokalani was her inspiration to study Ho'oponopono, and together with Nana Veary, studied with Morrnah Simeona, and Pali Jae Lee, ("Ho'opono"). Kumu Brenda extends love and gratitude always to Na Kumu Nana Veary, Aunty Margaret Machado, Pali Jae Lee, and Morrnah Simeona, among others.

It is Kumu Brenda's belief that in the sharing of some of the history and philosophy of ho'oponopono with grace and a genuinely caring heart, that others can awaken to and appreciate their own awareness of the healing power to "make things right." Kumu Brenda

17

guides participants to deepen their awareness and importance of bringing themselves to a place of being pono, (in balance) within and without, allowing passion for life and the healing power within to be ignited. Being pono is paramount to becoming a lomilomi practitioner. She invites all to claim the fulfillment, peace and joy that can come, according to one's belief and allowance.

Contact Kumu Brenda at bignacio808@aol.com

A NEW 50/50 WORLD

By Gill Whitty-Collins

I finished writing 'Why Men Win At Work' in March 2021, or thought I had; it already needed updating by the beginning of April as we started to see the impact of the pandemic on women and leadership across the world. Issues that have always been there were made visible and obvious and couldn't be ignored any longer.

Women have always generally carried the majority of the 'unpaid work' at home and for the family, even when they have paid work or a career of their own, but Covid and mandatory working from home, took this to a whole new level. Even more food shopping, meal preparation, housework and home-schooling on top. There simply aren't enough hours in the day to do everything and work too, let alone leaving enough time for some essential relaxation and a decent night's sleep.

It is no surprise that we saw research showing 1 in 4 women were considering giving up on their careers, altogether. And those who persevere are far more likely than men to leverage flexible work policies, because they need to and because many employers may have gender neutral policies on paper but most

19

don't in practice – the sexist assumption is that they are for women/mums not for men. And so we see women suffering the negative consequences of presenteeism and visibility bias (the Umbrella Theory!) while men are getting three times the promotions and double the salary increases.

The pandemic has been, quite simply, a disaster for feminism. We are even further away from gender equality than we were before and a very long way from seeing women equally leading our businesses, organizations, societies and our world. It is hard to believe that here we are, in 2022, with men still holding over 90% of the leadership positions in the world, while women still take most of the responsibility for running the home and family. Worse still, we are watching in despair as women lose the right to make decisions about their own bodies in the US and the right to wear the clothes they choose, and even to education in Afghanistan.

But I believe there is a positive. Gender inequality has always been an issue, we have never been close to true equality (even though many have had the deluded perception that we were) and this is now visible, obvious and unignorable in a way it never was before largely - thanks largely to the strength of women's presence on social media. Now that the inequality is so clear to see we can address it. And I feel a growing force of women who are ready to do that and are no longer willing to be positive, patient and polite about it. Women are 50% of the population and we have equal intelligence, and competence and I think we are done with accepting anything but equal rights and representation.

When we're living in normal, calm times it can be easy to under-estimate how important it is that too many women give up on their careers and leave men to take most of the leadership roles. But if there is one big lesson the last few years has taught us, it is that things go badly wrong when women aren't represented, or adequately represented in the room and at the table where important discussions are happening and key decisions are being made. I think it's pretty clear, for example, that a more gender balanced, diverse group would have discussed and foreseen the problems that closing schools and childcare facilities during the pandemic would lead to for women and for gender equality. That a better, smarter plan could have been constructed. Likewise, a more representative group would have been aware of the disproportionate impact on women that closing beauty salon and hairdressing businesses would have and would, I believe, have worked to find a smart, safe way to keep them open. In male-dominated leadership it is always male-focussed interests and issues that are prioritized.

This really isn't a difficult concept to grasp: when teams lack diversity they miss input and insights. They have incomplete discussions and make bad decisions. When teams are diverse and representative of the population, they benefit from the range of input, collective intelligence and better decisions that brings. This is why we need women, not just men, at the table and in leadership roles. This is why we must not accept anything that holds them back from being there.

One of the most obvious things we have seen over this time, in case any of us doubted it, is that women can lead! We have seen some simply amazing role model women in important leadership roles. For the first time, a woman, Kamala Harris, holds the role of Vice President of the US and we have no doubt when she says 'I may be the first, but I won't be the last'. Meanwhile, Angela Merkel continued and completed her reign as official Chancellor of Germany (and unofficial President of Europe!) and is universally acknowledged as one of the greatest leaders in the world. We also saw Jacinda Ardern emerge as possibly the most admired Head of State globally. She demonstrated a powerful combination of collaboration, listening, empathy, decisive and consistent action whilst remaining very clearly and authentically a woman and mother. Oh, and let's not forget, she and her husband have a 50/50 approach at home and for childcare: as she says 'he's a parent, not a babysitter'.

The emergence of some strong women leaders through the Covid crisis has led many to the pendulum-swing conclusion that women in fact are stronger leaders than men. This is rather simplistic in my view. I am certain, because I have seen and experienced it, that men are equally capable of all of the leadership traits we see in a Jacinda Ardern. These are not, however, necessarily the type of men that we have always chosen as our leaders. All too often we are so impressed by the confidence of a given man that we fail to notice that he may not be the most competent, rounded person for the job. We all love confident people, it is very human and natural to, but we always need to look behind the 'confident curtain' and see if there is real competence there. Or if there is another less confident but highly competent candidate (of whatever gender) that we have not seen, heard or noticed.

What we have seen is a number of brilliant women leaders who have overcome the gender barriers and made it to where they are because they have such a strong, rounded set of leadership skills. These women have been in a side-by-side comparison with some significantly less competent men leaders who have (or had) their position thanks to their confidence rather than for truly strong leadership abilities. The lesson is not that women are better leaders, it is that we need to choose our leaders wisely, whatever their gender.

Another lesson we need to learn if we want to see more women leading in our new world is the importance of authenticity. We have to say goodbye to the image that is deeply embedded in our consciousness of the leader as a man and we have to stop trying to 'fit' into or copy that, or expecting others to.

The key to success is to leverage the unique strengths and talents we have, we are never able to perform at our best if we are focusing on trying to do things the way someone else does. As Judy Garland said, 'Always be a first-rate version of yourself instead of a second-rate version of someone else.'

Not only will focusing on what we uniquely bring mean we will be performing at our best we will also, by definition, be authentic and this is so important. People can smell inauthenticity. They may not realize what it is but they have a feeling that there is something not quite right about someone, that they don't feel totally comfortable with them and that they can trust them. Feeling trust in someone is absolutely critical when you are considering giving them a leadership role, and authenticity is key to creating that trust. Ultimately women really have no other option but to show up authentically as themselves, even when it feels like we are very different from everyone around us, if we want to be chosen to lead.

At the same time, everyone has a responsibility to be aware of and swat away our unconscious bias that leadership looks like a man. The more female leader role models we see, the more it helps. That's why I loved the photo of Whitney Wolfe, CEO of Bumble, with her baby on her hip as her company went public and the sale raised $2 billion.

We have to get to the point where we recognize leadership whatever it looks like, whatever gender it is, whatever it is wearing, whatever voice or accent it has, whatever colour it is.

I really want to see women leading in our new world, but not just a few women, not just the few exceptions that hold 7% of the CEO roles or 9% of the Heads of State positions today. Women are 50% of the world's population, intelligence, competence and capability (including leadership ability). So for me this is very simple - I want to see them in 50% of the world's leadership roles. I'm not interested in a target of 30% or 40% of women on executive boards, why would we be content with that, why do we have such low expectations of women? Equality is 50/50 and anything less is sexist and patronizing.

Of course it's not easy to get there, we are a long way from it and we all (women and men) have a lot of work to do. This includes as a start point getting to true partnership and 50/50 at home: I am not aware of a single woman (or man, for that matter) on the planet who is carrying the unpaid work burden at home and holding a key leadership role. Nobody is doing it all. Nobody is doing everything perfectly. We don't expect this from men, so we must not expect it from women, including ourselves, either.

So many people have said this year that they wish they had a Jacinda Ardern leading their country. And I say they could have. There are Jacindas everywhere, we just often don't notice them. We don't value and encourage their unique strengths, or overwhelm them with so much to do that they don't have enough of themselves left for their career, so we don't choose them. We have a huge and ever growing supply of future women leaders, we need to take off the shackles and unleash them. Let's make our new world to be a 50/50 one, at home and at work.

About Gill Whitty-Collins

Gill Whitty-Collins is the author of 'Why Men Win at Work... and how we can make inequality history'. She was born near Liverpool in 1970, the youngest of three sisters. After attending the local  comprehensive high school she went on to study at Cambridge University. Upon graduating she joined Proctor and Gamble where she led global brands such as Olay, Always and Pantone.

She swiftly moved up the ladder to Marketing Director, General Manager and finally Senior Vice President. Her story and vision will inspire you to join the force to make gender inequality history. Gill now works as a keynote speaker, Consultant, Trainer and Executive Coach.

Contact Gill at www.gillwhittycollins.com

SHAPE YOUR LEADERSHIP FUTURE

By Helen Morphew

Nice girls don't get the corner office (Frankel, L. 2014) That was the title of the book I picked up from my boss's desk.

There are so many things wrong with this title I barely know where to start. But when I saw it sitting there on the bookshelf behind his desk in the corner office, I thought it was amusing. I was his head of Human Resources.

I gestured at the book, smiled then made a light-hearted comment about it being deeply inappropriate. His response was to give it to me.

When I started writing this chapter I looked for that book. It has followed me around over the years as a reminder of what I believe in. And importantly what I don't. But I must have given it away. It will now be sitting on another bookshelf for someone else to smirk at.

I never did get around to reading the book. I have no idea if it was positive or negative, thoughtful or superficial, I don't really care, but it was the title that drew me and got me thinking; what does it take to get that corner office?

I really enjoyed working with this particular boss. HR is a female dominated environment, but I'd chosen to pursue this particular career in the male dominated financial services environment. Normally at the time my HR leader would be female and my business leader would be male. I had made a conscious decision with this role to work for a man. A few bad experiences with female leaders had left their mark.

It makes me sad to write that.

I feel that delving deeply into the details doesn't gain anything. Suffice to say that several of my female leaders had chosen to lead by emulating negative alpha traits. Leading through aggression or coercion.

I started to reflect on the other leaders I had witnessed and been exposed to through work, not just the ones I reported to. I'd experienced the behaviours of aggression and coercion from both men and women. The power games played through belittling team members, making them feel inadequate, shouting in public. To me it wasn't a leadership style that I enjoyed being around, regardless of whether I was the target.

I tried to identify some of the traits of these leaders and, whilst conscious of generalising, found a number of similarities regardless of gender. The positive leaders were empowering, encouraging, inspiring, visioning. And the less positive leaders were dictatorial "my way" leaders, micromanaging or ineffective. In common I noticed that a surprising number of both had struggled when it came to addressing conflict within their teams.

But what do I mean by a leader?

In an organisational setting a leader is in a position of authority with the title, salary and responsibility to match. Not just the CEO who is undoubtedly a leader, but also the heads of teams, subject matter experts, managers, heads of department etc. Ultimately, a leader's role is one that people look up to, some aspire to. It's a position of influence.

But what makes them positive leaders?

Some of the female leaders I've experienced were truly inspirational. One of my very first HR leaders for example had a reputation for being pretty fierce but wow, she was fair. I learnt so much from her. She now has an OBE so I'm not alone in thinking how impressive she is. What did she do that was so inspiring? She supported me. She asked me what I needed from her. She facilitated my growth and learning. Occasionally she reigned me in, but she gave me as much responsibility as I could manage, and she somehow knew how much that was.

My work now as a coach with aspiring and existing leaders is informed by these positive experiences. After all, our experiences shape us.

I recently had a coaching session where my client was mulling over the question about what it takes to be a leader. Her view was that leadership involved coaching, mentoring, being able to stand up in the midst of a crisis and to cope. These were all things she acknowledged she was good at and had the skills and aptitude for. 'What else?', I asked her. 'Assertiveness and dealing with conflict', was her reply but as she said this she visibly flinched and screwed herself up. 'I really hate that stuff', she said.

And she's not alone. In response to her reaction, I felt my own palms get sweaty.

We assume that being assertive or dealing with conflict is negative. How many times have you heard someone say they don't like conflict or confrontation, and empathised with them? Some people do enjoy it but in my experience, these are the minority. But is this aversion holding us back from that metaphorical corner office, or whatever our own goals may be?

Perhaps.

It used to hold me back. Or rather my thinking held me back.

At one company I was asked to set up a professional female networking group. We invited heads of businesses and inspirational speakers, men and women, to talk and share their stories. As we left our desks to attend the meetings we would be followed by shouts of 'Can I come if I wear a skirt?', or 'What are you all going to talk about?', and 'It's not fair, we want an all-male networking group'.

Our response was always the same, please come along.

So what was the point of the group? In a predominantly male environment, it was about providing support, about normalising. It's not about repelling the opposite sex, but it's acknowledging we're different and we need different things. It's not about exclusivity but about inclusivity.

Having worked for many years in HR, firstly in London and then in New Zealand, I finally decided to leave the corporate world. Subsequently as a business owner in New Zealand in a slightly obscure field, I was fortunate enough to be invited to a female networking group for a related industry. These women were business owners and specialists, and some were just starting out. The two things they had in common, their gender and their field. The group provided me not only with an opportunity for business networking but networking in general. It also provided support. Being new to the industry, they helped me navigate some of the complexities. I hosted speakers to build knowledge and on a more informal level the group provided a safe place for discussion and sharing of thoughts, concerns and ideas.

We don't exist in a bubble and in terms of leadership we shouldn't need to. Whether a networking group is for you or not, there are a myriad of other ways you can access inspiration. Many other sources exist to help you to lead in the way you want to.

TED Talks, inspirational and motivational speakers, podcasts, documentaries, masterclasses, books (paper, electronic or audible), formal courses and coaching, to name but a few. Some of the material is media based, some interpersonal and some is individualised. Some free, some not. I encourage you to tap into whichever mode works for you, or a selection of them.

I said before that our experiences shape us, but that shape is a work in progress, it does not need to be the final product. Don't let it hold you back.

Certain behaviours or circumstances can trigger us. It is important to recognise that and then work with that thought or feeling. We can work on ourselves; we can learn and we can work out what our values are so that we're being real and authentic and true to ourselves.

To the leader who forbade me from going to lunch with my colleague, 'Because you always get lunch together and that's not a good look', I would now laugh. I would not compromise my values. The directive said so much more about that leader than it did about me or my colleague.

But what is my overall message?

In whatever you do, be true to yourself.

As a leader I encourage you to lead courageously, with authenticity. Be a powerfully constructive leader and do it in the way you want to. Use your platform to give others the opportunity to excel. Look for inspiring leaders, male or female, who fit with your own values and style, and emulate those positive characteristics. All with your own spin, obviously.

Whether you support her political stance or not, few people disagree that the New Zealand Prime Minister, Jacinda Ardern, has been a pretty remarkable leader in the face of a global pandemic. But why? What do you think? The answer is personal. My answer won't be your answer, my reasons aren't your reasons, so, have a think.

There is no need to be 'nice' but there is also no need to turn yourself into someone you're not, to get that corner office. Not everyone wants to be a leader in the old fashioned sense of the word. We can all lead with actions and words, but whatever your leadership medium, be real. Be who you are.

Become the best you can be and be curious. Be your own best advocate and don't be afraid to surround yourself with people who are more skilled than you, who complement your abilities and support your 'gaps' in knowledge, experience or whatever.

Taking inspiration from Anna Wintour, I invite you to think about who you are, how you lead, and own that without apology

(Frankel, L., 2014.) Nice girls don't get the corner office; Business Plus

About **Helen Morphew**

Helen is an accredited ICF Coach with an extensive background in senior strategic human resource management across the financial, insurance and professional services industries, as well as small business ownership. She supports women so that they can lead from a place of authenticity, and thrive, in fast paced, high pressure environments.

Her style is pragmatic, and she takes a non-directive approach enabling her clients to step back and observe - rather than continuing habitual reactions - to create lasting change. She is focused on results, and is a believer in expanding strengths and building confidence to deliver sustainable outcomes.

Her clients may be experiencing a career transition or facing significant challenge; she also provides coaching for those who might be leaving an organisation, helping them shape their future aspirations and direction. She regularly works with those looking to become unstuck, create their own change, increase confidence, and shift unhelpful thinking patterns.

If she can support you, or your organisation, Helen would love to hear from you.

LinkedIn:
https://www.linkedin.com/in/helenmorphew/

Email: helen@ashahousecoaching.com

Website: www.ashahousecoaching.com

TIME TO WAKE UP – THE REAL MEANING OF CONSCIOUS LEADERSHIP

By Sara Sabin

For as long as I can remember I felt that I possessed 'masculine' traits. They were the traits that I told myself I needed to develop to succeed in the world. They were the qualities I felt were needed to silence the people that bullied me when I was young.

At primary school I was so shy that I could hardly speak but I always pushed myself harder and harder. If someone told me I couldn't do something I would go to tremendous lengths to prove them wrong.

Being always surrounded by people that I perceived to be smarter than me further fuelled that competition and drive. My whole identity was constructed around the idea of needing to subdue my femininity to succeed. I told myself I needed to quieten my intuition, my strengths as a communicator and influencer, and my empathy.

This cycle was perpetuated throughout my years in the corporate world. Frequently I remember being the only woman in a room full of directors. I remember talented women missing out on promotion. I remember that the women I saw in power also showed typically 'masculine' traits.

By the time I entered the start-up world and founded my own tech start-up my ideas of leadership were formed. I fully admit that I was a nightmare to work for – no one could live up to my high expectations. I spent much of my time trying to push people into doing things. I did not set clear boundaries or communication (I didn't have the time for that!) so there was no cohesion in the way I led a team. There was no inspirational camaraderie and I believed I had to be aggressive to get things done. The behaviour was unconscious and I felt I was continually putting on a mask and pushing. I was constantly exhausted.

The interesting thing was that I did not take responsibility for my leadership style. I blamed problems on other people and on circumstances. I have learned since then that the only way to create true lasting transformation is to take responsibility for everything that happens in your life. Be aware of your part in everything that happens. See the gift and the lesson in everything then you can choose to behave differently.

In my conversations with hundreds of leaders the 'conscious ones' had guidance and mentoring from a good leader. They saw the positive effects of that guidance before adopting it for themselves as a leadership style.

In the absence of great leaders in our immediate environment it can be easy to resort to thinking that you have not got what it takes to lead. Or you can choose to put on a mask.

It takes courage to envision another way, and to take the time to find out who you are as a person and as an authentic leader. If you can do so you will tap into your greater motivations. You will start to see a picture bigger than just yourself and your own personal and company's advancement.

How do I become more conscious?

So much of the time we, as humans, need to reach some kind of breaking point to change. Years of chronic stress, anxiety and being on the brink of burn-out did it for me. I knew that I could achieve even more and reach higher potential but I knew what I had been doing was not the path for me to get there. I needed to incorporate all aspects of who I was, the masculine and the feminine side. All of us need that balance whether we are a man or a woman.

Through coaching I woke up to myself. I found a strong purpose and my WHY. I started to peel back all of the layers of who I was. I began to find out more about myself and discover my greatest strengths, and who I was as a leader. It took courage. I faced my shadow side and my demons. But from that place I found my mission which was so much bigger than just me. I found my moonshot: the bigger impact that I want to make in the world.

Although, conscious leadership can cross over into the spiritual if you are so inclined, it is, at an extremely simplistic level, about 'being self-aware'. The better we know ourselves the more sure we can be of our actions and decisions and our true motivations for doing them. We can then understand other people better which has a knock-on effect in motivating them.

Conscious leadership encourages introspection rather than jumping in to improve or fix the outside. The outside action is important but when it comes from a place of new understanding it takes on an added dimension. It also creates a bigger impact.

Self-awareness is the very core foundation of emotional intelligence, the often talked about cherry on the cake. This foundation creates star-performing leaders as opposed to average and technically perfect ones.

The old paradigm and perception of companies being 100% focused on making money at the expense of their workforce and the planet are outdated.

Everything is inextricably intertwined. It's time we started to associate being 'good and fair' with 'good business' and profitable business. To have a more profitable business, the key to the equation lies in unlocking human potential and purpose and creating more conscious leaders. It is the key to innovation, to customer service, to engagement.

The stick method will not buy you loyalty or an employee's best work. It is short term thinking.

Conscious leadership represents an unprecedented opportunity to succeed in business by bucking the trend. The more conscious we are the more we apply 'future intelligence' where we make decisions from a place of thriving and considering the future consequences of our actions and for all parties. For ourselves, our company and the planet. Good for one, good for all.

Think about what a different world we might have if leaders became more conscious. War, competition, greed, and lack of empathy have got us to where we are. We cannot get ourselves out of this state by continuing to think and act in a way that we always have. Fresh leadership is needed.

How do you develop conscious leadership?

The first step on the road to becoming a conscious leader is to develop self-awareness as to who you are, where your strengths lie, your Vision and Purpose. This also forms the foundations for developing greater emotional intelligence. When I work with clients, I encourage them to think of transformation, as starting from the inside out, following a framework for change. Know yourself, know that which you want to create and start creating those steps in the outside world.

Know your compelling vision

If you don't know what your vision is and your big WHY, as both a human being and a leader, how can you hope to inspire others? Your vision gives you a clear direction. Yes, obstacles will inevitably come up but with a clear vision you simply change the steps you need to get there. People that buy into your vision can begin to have a clear sense of their own purpose. Purpose is a powerful motivator if communicated in a transparent way and it creates a shared philosophy. Do that successfully and you have a team of people working towards a common vision, in alignment with their personal purpose, rather than each one following their own agenda.

Identity

Stop trying to be something you're not. If your way of leading feels draining to you it's a sign that what you are doing is probably not working for you. If you are not getting the results you want from yourself and others reflect and think why that is. Take the time to ask yourself the big questions: who are you, what is your purpose and are you acting in alignment with it? What are your core values that need to filter through into everything that you do? Are you leading in a way that feels right for you? Maybe not everyone will agree with you but you will have a better chance of inspiring others who strongly resonate with you. Authenticity creates loyalty and trust.

Inspire Others by Owning up to your Failures and Vulnerabilities

Time and again I've heard employees say that they cannot see themselves in their leaders. They seem remote and inaccessible like they have transcended a level beyond that of 'the rest of us'. This helps with authoritarian leadership, sure but I would argue it's not long-term thinking.

We are all human. Showing your human side as a leader is not a sign of weakness, it is the ultimate strength. Admitting your failures, your mistakes, your bad decisions and talking about what you have learned is important in developing leadership skills in your team. It allows you to destigmatize the notion of failure. It helps you to build a culture of leaders who are engaged, responsible and accountable for their own and their company's success.

Set a strategy and action plan for the type of leader that you want to be.

Rather than boxing yourself into a 'personality type' know the type of leader that you want to embody and start holding yourself accountable to that. Ask yourself powerful questions to make yourself more aware of how you are acting in any given circumstance. And in the same way, as if you were training to run a marathon, set yourself small consistent action steps that take you closer to your goal every day. When you fall off the wagon, simply get up and start again.

Developing an Agile Mindset

The highest performers in the world know that learning is never done. Experience is crucial, but it can be a double-edged sword. If you stop learning and growing and instead rely on previous experience, and apply only your experience to all new situations, you may lose the ability to adapt to change when required. Everything is changing all the time. More so in today's world. As Donald Rumsfeld once said, "you can't know what you don't know." Through being conscious of the limits of your knowledge and being humble, you can truly excel, as learning becomes part of your DNA.

"Until you make the unconscious conscious, it will direct your life and you will call it fate." Carl Jung

I invite you, the readers, to start awakening.

About Sara Sabin

Sara Sabin is a qualified accountant, former start-up founder, leadership coach and consultant, as well as a regular contributor for Entrepreneur Magazine and the Fast Company. She is on a mission to change  how we perceive leadership, and to accelerate the trend towards conscious leadership. For conscious leaders, it is about embracing both our masculine and feminine sides, whatever our gender.

She believes that purpose and profit are intertwined and that by focusing on impact and service, it leads not only to higher satisfaction but ultimately, more profit. Sara partners with innovative companies and entrepreneurs, to coach leaders, and their teams, to become more emotionally smart, focused and higher performing, and to approach business challenges in a more creative way, so that they are more effective, impactful and satisfied at work. Find out more at www.SaraSabin.com – The Underpreneur and Sara Caroline Sabin on LinkedIn.

LEADERSHIP HAS NEVER BEEN JUST FOR THE WISE OLD OWLS

By Beverley Ann Shrimpling

I grew up amid contrasting vistas, the picturesque rolling hills and heather moorlands of North Yorkshire, and the smouldering Industrial heartland of 1970's North East England. Racism was ripe, the North South economic divide was palpable, inequality for women was par for the course and LGBTQ+ rights were barely out the starting gate. I lived in a mid-sized, primarily white town with cobbled streets, leafy hills just steps from my front door, and slightly unhealthy beaches a short, cigarette-filled bus ride away. My parents had broken into the middle class and it was the beginning of a consumer boom; package holidays, two car families, more than one TV in a home, microwave meals, VHS recorders etc. My parents rarely read newspapers, but religiously watched the six and nine o'clock news, and together we watched prime time TV as a family on weekends. Although my parents emerged from the sixties with more liberal views than my grandparent's generation, my dad was extremely conservative and my mum was apolitical.

In comparison to today's rapid information at our fingertips, my early sources of women leaders and women's history in general was limited to four TV channels, a modest library, a lacking national curriculum and my personal interactions with family and friends. My mother was an energetic Keep Fit Association teacher and my great aunt a fiercely independent matriarch, both leaders in their own right. However, in spite of their influence, life in a white, middle class, gender stereotypical household did not stir a thirst, or a need for me to consider leadership as a priority in my early years. I didn't associate female fashion, music or acting icons as leaders in any way.

My schools were generally headed up by men; the chemist, the supermarket manager, the grocer, the butcher, all men. Even during my Kate Adie obsession, the exceptional, ground-breaking war correspondent that I pretended to be, reporting from the frontline in my pink heart themed bedroom, a hairbrush as my microphone, a torch balanced on my bed for that dramatic night time effect; even Kate in my mind might be a great reporter, but would surely have a male boss telling her what to do. From the representation and influence of those around me, my youthful mindset was that leaders were only those people at the very top of the hierarchy and they were predominantly male. Women leaders were these wise old owls that emerged after decades of experience, and that any political female giants were privately educated and had been on that path from birth, such as Margaret Thatcher, Benazir Bhutto and Indira Ghandi. I was the product of my environment and I was wrong.

Over forty years before I would witness Kate Adie's suspense filled reporting, at the age of only sixteen, an intelligent and spirited Sophie Scholl was experiencing her first Gestapo interrogation. Five years later she would face the ultimate test of courage. After recognising the lies of the Third Reich, Sophie, then a university student, joined her brother's resistance group The White Rose. Their aim was to stir fellow students and influential Germans into action.

Using peaceful methods of propaganda, The White Rose called out the atrocities being carried out in Germany's name and voiced the reality that the war was being lost. Knowing that a single word uttered against the Nazi regime could result in death, this was young leadership at a perilous level. In 1942, Sophie and her brother were arrested while dropping leaflets in their university and charged with treason. Mindful of her age, the Gestapo officer tried to give Sophie a way out by suggesting she was acting under the influence of her older brother. But even at twenty-one, Sophie's core values and personal conviction reigned. They had been cemented through the experience of living under tyranny. They would not permit her to concede to this opportunity to escape by denying her convictions.

She spoke unashamedly about why their actions were necessary and fully accepted the consequences. Just four days after their arrest, Sophie, Hans and their friend Christoph were tried by the highest court without any legal support. They were murdered by guillotine, the very same day. QUOTE from Sophie?

Sophie's strength of character in life, and resolution in death, has been so inspirational to me that I am in the process of writing a novel so I can continue to share her remarkable story.

These days, the internet and social media have enabled so many young female leaders to burst into the spotlight, often swiftly and internationally. These women are demonstrating the true diversity of leadership that has always existed but which is now accessible in real time, and in a manner generations before simply did not have. Imagine being able to follow Sophie Scholl on Twitter? Often these young mentors initially do not pursue global exposure, but choose to step up when their values are overwhelmingly challenged.

All are compelled by profound beliefs, fortified by personal experiences, and they share the goal of driving positive change; Malala Yousafzai, Sophie Cruz, Emma Gonzalez, Shamma bint Suhail Faris

Mazrui, Greta Thunberg, Nupol Kiazolu, Amanda Gorman, to name but a few. These young women fearlessly speak their truth, often under daily threats and abuse from those who would prefer they close their mouths and sit quietly in a corner.

Sophie Scholl once said "The real damage is done by those millions who want to 'survive.' The honest men who just want to be left in peace. Those who don't want their little lives disturbed by anything bigger than themselves. Those with no sides and no causes. Those who won't take measure of their own strength, for fear of antagonising their own weakness. Those who don't like to make waves—or enemies. Those for whom freedom, honour, truth, and principles are only literature. Those who live small, mate small, die small. It's the reductionist approach to life: if you keep it small, you'll keep it under control. If you don't make any noise, the bogeyman won't find you. But it's all an illusion, because they die too, those people who roll up their spirits into tiny little balls so as to be safe. Safe?! From what? Life is always on the edge of death; narrow streets lead to the same place as wide avenues, and a little candle burns itself out just like a flaming torch does. I choose my own way to burn."

Making our voices heard has become imperative for more than just the progression of gender and racial equality. How we choose to burn our flame matters as women's rights continue to be in danger, our planet is being abused and even the most secure democracies seem vulnerable.

In my late teens after entering the workforce and joining the Army Reserves, I soon learned that leadership was not just for wise old owls, and the road to success as a woman could start at any age. That it could be frustrating, occasionally soul destroying and dotted with many moments of isolation, but was ultimately incredibly rewarding. Through these relentless challenges, I discovered my own deep-rooted compass.

My powerful internal governance determined what standards I was prepared to fight for, which ethics I was prepared to leave a job for, and which principles I was unwilling to break. I wasn't shattering glass ceilings daily, or leading a global movement, but I recognised I had become part of a centuries old legion of women, whittling away at collective objectives. Even though at times it felt like walking uphill through dry sand, onward we marched!

Social media has without doubt made women's issues harder to ignore, and become a tool to enable millions of women to stand as one mighty roar. We must utilise these tools that connect us, use them to elevate the many whispered stories of women leaders of past and present; stories that can motivate us and renew our spirits. We must continue to be inspired by the confidence of our young women influencers, who have used their determination and the tools of their generation to force the patriarchy and international governments to sit up and listen. We must also recognise, and be just as proud of, the single mum who advocates for her daughter's education; or the grandmother who starts a new career; or the group of young teens who stand up to racism on the train; or the mum that petitions for flexible work schedules; or the trans teacher who brings courage into her classroom; and all women who steer the sisterhood forward in discreet, gentle ways.

It took time for me to grasp the true variety of women's leadership, to recognise that it is essential to collective progress, and to benefit the world we inhabit.

I believe we are finally being primed for the mass empowerment of exceptional women leaders, I believe our planet and our societies desperately need this. It is imperative that each of us not only make our own contributions, but that we proactively light the fires in the bellies of our daughters, and all young women universally, without delay.

Fellow sister, I encourage you to stay the course, discover and embrace your core values, continue to be a force for positive change, support other women, inspire our future warriors and as Sophie Scholl once said, "Stand up for what you believe in, even if you are standing alone."

About Beverley Ann Shrimpling

Exhausted mum, fearless feminist and all-round defender of the mistreated. Raised in North Yorkshire during the turbulent Thatcher years, an Army Reservist at nineteen, Beverley balanced successful military and  civilian careers. She married an American in Scotland, spending the conflicting Bush/Obama years in the USA.

Beverley achieved several firsts for women in her Regiment and Brigade, was a founding member of Women in Defence, Michigan and relished being part of the global phenomena that was the 2016 Women's March. Having returned once again to old blighty, to the historic lands of Mercia, Beverley draws from her collective life experiences in her writing. She has long appreciated the tenacity, courage and emotional force of women. Beverley's desire to tell amazing women's stories has led to the start of a book based on the remarkable life of Sophie Scholl, the young German White Rose resistance fighter murdered by the Third Reich.

Facebook: /BAShrimpling

WOMEN LEADING IN THE NEW AGE, SHINE YOUR UNEARTHLY LIGHT!

By Eva Maria Hunt

"You are special to be, as you are, Eva, because you have natural abilities tuned within you. There is such a genuine, real pull towards you." Sara, New York

Most people cruise through life, thinking they must fit in. There is a certain level of comfort in feeling like they are part of the crowd. It gives a sense of support, safety and security. However, if you were born to be a leader, soon you realise it is uncomfortable to repress yourself. So you try to fix things within you, thinking there is something wrong with you.

If you feel like a black sheep i.e. you don't belong, even when you are surrounded by your loving, blood family, chances are you were born to stand out.

The question is what to do with this discovery: HIDE, because you feel like a weirdo; or SHINE like a star? I have done both.

I am sharing my story with you in the hope that it will inspire you to connect with your soul, to align with your true purpose, so you can fly your freak flag. This is the work I have been doing with my clients for the last 11 years. I am a multi-passionate creative, so during this last decade or so, different facets of me got polished, therefore I was shining brighter and brighter, whilst becoming more confident in my own abilities.

The very first step I took on this path was to become a hands-on healer, Reiki practitioner and crystal healer in 2010. It was a real challenge for me, as many people were looking at me as a weirdo. Considering that my original profession is commercial economist, I was well out of my comfort zone. I shifted from science-based, logical living, and complying with the masculine standards of society, to fully trusting my intuition's guidance and unleashing my inner feminine.

When I got a bit more comfortable with being seen, as someone different, I was ready for the next step. Teaching Qigong, a Chinese self-healing art, was pushing me even further away from what the world considered, as normal and acceptable. I wanted to learn this healing modality, so my clients could take away something that could always help and empower them.

In 2015 my journey continued with me becoming a self-taught artist, as my psychic abilities were breaking through. Channelling Reiki and paintings with messages from above, were still not as scary, as what I knew I have been protecting within me all this time.

I was actively searching for answers by then. I knew that if you live your passion, the Universe fully supports you. In my case it was like a roller coaster ride. Support full-on and then no support at all. I didn't understand why.

During the time I have been working in the holistic healing arena, I became better and better at aligning with the Universe.

I was aware that the Cosmos, the energies surrounding us, have constantly been changing. In December 2020 we stepped into the Age of Aquarius. This is the start of a new era, when we can make a choice to create a better world. By shifting from materialistic views of the world and separation i.e. it is mine! to a cultural shift of sharing, unity and collaboration. So, if you are wondering how this change on the Quantum Level is helping you to become a leader, here is your answer.

You are made of energy. You are the alchemist, the creator of your life. And The Age of Aquarius is providing you with all the help you need. There is your own intuition to guide you for starters, and many spirit beings and angels, i.e. your own spirit team is ready to assist you. However, you must have an open mind! You must accept that you have a mortal and an immortal side to you, you are spirit with a human body.

Connecting with your soul is giving you all the guidance, power, and inspiration you need to step out into the limelight. Sounds simple! But the difficulty is to face your deepest fears, like I did.

It all started with me announcing to my husband, after many years of trying to make our marriage work, that I wanted a divorce. The only problem with that was, at that time my business couldn't provide me with a steady flow of income. I panicked and was looking for jobs that offered financial security. I knew I could do so many things with my university degree and decades of experience in management positions, but I wasn't even invited in for an interview. In the process I discovered that if I couldn't live my passion i.e. continue with my business, there is no meaning for my life. I got to a point where I didn't know the answers anymore. There was one way ahead, to surrender to the Universe.

And this was it. At one of the darkest times of my life, out of the blue, the Universe answered my prayers and stepped in, to make me face my biggest fear of all, so I could make it over the finishing line and become the leader I am today.

In January 2020 I connected with someone on social media who was talking about the subjects of raising consciousness and shifting into a higher frequency of being. It was right up my street, so we started conversing. It all led to an opportunity to sign up for a three-month spiritual course, which promised to deliver healing on the deepest level for the participants. There was also an opportunity to learn the techniques used, offering a chance to become a spiritual counsellor/coach.

The only problem was, I couldn't afford even the lowest tier of participation. It turned out that the guy I was chatting with, was one of the facilitators for the course, so he offered me a scholarship, if I was able to pay a quarter of the investment. Guess what! That was almost the exact amount of money in my bank account. I knew deep inside that it was a make-or-break situation. So, I said yes.

I had no idea, when I signed up to that 3 week after the course started, that the pandemic would create an unprecedented situation, or that a lockdown would begin on 23rd March 2020.

On that very day it dawned on me the Universe really was on my side. I realised I didn't get any of the jobs I have applied for, for a very good reason. I couldn't move out, as planned, because I wouldn't be able to support myself on my own, living in quarantine.

I did pay the price for my safety in a way, that I was on lockdown for 5 months with my husband I was divorcing. The most important thing was that I had a roof over my head, I was fed and watered. On top of that I was very grateful for being held in a safe place emotionally by 4 course facilitators and connected with 30 members of my newly found soul family, as fellow students, online.

It was very tough, I won't lie. I did make amazing progress though. Firstly, and most importantly I have managed to break through the last barriers to living from my heart i.e., from unconditional love. Secondly, I have found the missing link, the very answer I was looking for.

Your soul is always emitting light – unearthly light – that makes you stand out. You have your unique energies supporting your soul mission. However, if you keep hiding behind your ego, you can only sink into the ordinary and will be unable to take advantage of all the support of the Universe showering you constantly.

Look within! What are you taking for granted that you are brilliant at? What is it inside of you that makes you who you are? You must connect with your unearthly light, your weirdo nature, so you can shine!

For me it was my ability to channel. When I learned to channel Reiki, I didn't feel anything at the beginning. Only my Reiki master and my case study clients were telling me how amazing the experience was for them. Years later, one of my psychic friends pointed out, I have a strong connection with angels, so I should channel messages through drawings and paintings from them. I thought she was joking. I was very sceptical about it. And when I realised I could do it, I didn't value it. I thought everyone could do this. These abilities were so natural for me I just couldn't see them as something special.

In 2020, when I was pushed on my knees to face myself and who I truly was, I realised I have been a sensitive intuitive in my whole life. I didn't believe in myself though. So, I set a tough challenge. If I could connect with people from all over the world, just through an email and could conduct 10 blind readings, i.e. only knowing the person's name and one question they wanted an answer for, I will accept I am good. I got 9 ratings submitted for the 10 readings. One was only a two star one, however eight readings came back with an astonishing 5-star rating in varying subjects.

As a result, I have discovered that channelling is my thing. It is what I am good at. My psychic abilities, which I was guarding with my life, hiding away, not wanting to be seen as even more of a weirdo, were the missing link.

I became a YouTuber, helping strong women, who were brilliant at their job and life in general. But, these same survivor skills made them unable to attract their match in love.

These videos caught the attention of a mediumship company, looking for new readers. They reached out to me, offering an interview for the job, which I got on the spot. This was the Universe's way to give me a final proof that I was really meant to do this type of work.

Parallel with this new job, I was building up my channel, using all of my skills, wisdom, and knowledge I had gathered in the last decade. It turned out that my psychic abilities were the glue to all the different facets I was polishing before, as a healer, law of attraction and consciousness coach, teacher and spiritual guide. Even my channelled paintings got incorporated in my online general love readings, as I was guided to create an oracle deck from them and use them for connecting with people's souls.

YouTube became my lead generation tool, to bring in reading clients, who I could convert into coaching ones. Three months after the course finished, I was earning 'proper' money, and I managed to move out. One year on, I am fully supported by the Universe. I am living my mission, my passion as a leader of a hub for twin flames and light workers.

Perceiving yourself the right way is key. It's like seeing the glass half full or half empty. When, not long ago, I realised that the word weird means unearthly, I have changed overnight from a weirdo, who is seen as different and less than others, to a WEIRD-O, who is unique, rare to come across, proud to SHINE her unearthly light. O, being a circle, stands for completion and unity. To unite people with their soul, and leading people to unity, as opposed to separation.

About Eva Maria Hunt

Eva Maria Hunt is a Multi-passionate Creative, Executive Contributor for Brainz Magazine, Consciousness Coach and Soul Alchemist, helping people to connect with their soul to love and thrive .

After successfully beating depression, Eva's mission became to help strong women to connect within, in order to move forward. For more than a decade she has been combining her intuitive skills with Law of Attraction principles, energy healing and spirituality to guide those in need and empower them.

Eva's original profession is commercial economist, which is as far away from being an energy healer, as her native country, Hungary, from her adopted one, the UK.

Her channelled paintings are emotionally moving and perfect for meditation. Some of them were published in VIBE book, in which she also contributed to, as one of the 'colour experts'.

Her YouTube channel, 'Moon Goddess Oracle, Journey to 5D' provides guidance in love for twin flames and soulmates. Contact Eva at www.spiritual-wonders.com

HOLIDAY SNAPS DON'T INSPIRE

By Peter Turley

Imagine the scene - you have been invited to a friend's home for a dinner party. You're really looking forward to it and you can't wait to share with them and the other friends your wonderful news.

The big day arrives and as you spend time in front of the mirror, trying on several outfits to find the one that will make you look and feel amazing, you're running through the mental checklist of all the things you mustn't forget to share during the evening.

Well, dinner turns out to be delicious, so you decide that your news can wait until afterwards, so you can (a) enjoy the fabulous food, and (b) make sure that nobody else is distracted from your news by all the wonderful flavours.

After an hour or so of polite small talk, the dishes are cleared and coffee is poured. Here it comes, the time for proper conversation. You're sipping away, doing that final run through the checklist in your head, but before you can say anything, the hostess makes an announcement, "You must all see the photographs of myself and Tom's holiday".

And so begins the most butt-clenching cringeworthy hour of your life. "Here we are at the Pyramids. Here we are halfway up the Pyramids. Here's Tom in his swimming costume. Oh, and look, here we are at the top of the Pyramids. OMG you should have seen the view, you simply must go!"

Yes, you say to yourself, I simply must go alright, home to bed. The first moment you can make your excuses and get away with ordering a cab.

Sound familiar?

We've all been there at some point or other, haven't we?

You see, when we are part of a group of people, be it socially or professionally, and the conversation becomes all about one person and all the things they've done and all the things they've achieved for themselves, it can make us feel quite small, insignificant, and even resentful. And the longer it goes on the smaller and more insignificant, more resentful we can feel.

Whatever the reason they have for turning the conversation to themselves and dominating it, they have detracted themselves and forgotten it is a conversation, not a monologue. It can in fact be very uninspiring to the rest of us at the table.

The reason I bring this up is this - how often do we see our so-called leaders stand up to the microphone at the company AGM or the Political Party Conference, behaving in exactly this kind of manner? It's almost as if, by speaking like this, they deserve to be the leader because they are so much better and so wonderful. Almost like the rest of us are so underwhelming in comparison, we wouldn't be able to do anything without them.

This kind of thing never inspires much in the way of progress or greatness in this world.

So, what's the lesson here?

I believe the lesson here is that the people we are leading can often be so stuck in the way of doing things the way they have always done them, because that's the way they were shown how to do it when they started out, and it's really hard to break them out of a habit. They keep doing the same, even when it makes more sense to adopt a new and better way. The reason for this can often be the inbuilt human fear of change.

To break habits, to try new things, to get over their fears, people have to be inspired to try things for themselves, not told to do it by someone else because they did something once, a long time ago. There is a gulf of a difference between one and the other. So, it is critically important to learn how to create an atmosphere where people believe in themselves and believe in what they can achieve.

Imagine the power of being able to inspire people to try new things. Imagine the potential of making the world a better and more sustainable place to be.

How do you do it?

Well, you don't do it by talking about leadership. You don't do it by adding 'leadership' to your mission statement. You don't do it by talking about how many followers you have on Facebook or LinkedIn or Instagram, and you certainly don't do it by teaching people how to get likes and shares on social media, not even by just reading books on leadership, like this one.

You do it by being creative and inspiring as a leader yourself. By standing up and showing them how it's done. Because people are 'inspired' into action by watching others doing great things. They look at someone else doing something inspirational and they say, "If she can do that, then I can do it too."

So, please think about this, write it down if you need to: "What is the most inspiring thing I have done up until now? What is the most inspiring thing I could do as a leader today? What is the most inspiring thing I could do as a leader tomorrow? And what is the most inspiring thing I could do as a leader next week?"

You seem to be inspirational, you must understand that the word inspirational comes from the verb 'inspire' which means, to fill with an animated, quickened or exalted influence. "Her courage inspired her followers to achieve incredible outcomes".

And you will never inspire people more than when you create a sense that you are there with them, going through it with them, that you are there in the trenches, holding their hands; and when it comes time for action, you'll be there with them, every step of the way.
Inspiration is a sense of being, not of telling, and we are never closer to our true purpose in life than when we are inspiring other people to be the very best that they can be. When we show them that we can sense the real qualities in them. Then they will believe in what they can achieve, for themselves and those around them.

I urge you to develop your ability to stand up and show people the greatness within, so that you may inspire those around you to achieve their true potential. Because that is how we will create a better and more sustainable world for all.

Good luck with that.

About Peter Turley

Peter Turley is an author and award-winning sales speaker and trainer. His company, Sell Squared, based in Dublin, Ireland, specialises in teaching business owners what it takes to outshine  competitors, weather recessions, build profitable businesses, raise strong and fiercely loyal teams, and earn their reputation as "The one that does what it takes to be the very best".

Contact Peter at www.sellsquared.com

WHAT'S LOVE GOT TO DO WITH IT?

By Tania Adams

There is one commonality that all human beings share, it's internalised and externalised, demonstrated through human expression and tangible objects, it heals and transforms, it supports and encourages, it's nurturing and nourishing, it empowers and energises, it keeps us safe, it grows and expands, and it has no expiry date. It creates miracles, it's a feeling, it's a gift and it's our innate true nature which is otherwise known as LOVE! Everyone wants to be loved, feel loved and love and through the notion of love we feel whole and complete. There is tremendous power in love, in fact, I would say it's the most powerful ingredient, human emotion, self-expression, superpower, lifeforce and it's alive and here on earth.

Throughout my life I have grown to understand, accept and embrace both the gift and power of love and through this realisation, I have embodied and witnessed great change and transformation not just from my own experience, but from other people and the world at large. What's interesting about love is that everyone wants it, and everyone has it, but they may not know how to access it, demonstrate it or be with it and this all depends on our life experience and connection to our true self. As human beings, we often strive for money and luxurious living to give us more fulfilment and this is all great, however, what if we also strived for love to fulfil us and create harmony which doesn't cost anything! If everyone in the world really knew the power that prevails from this magic potion, we'd be living in a different level of consciousness.

In our world today and now more than ever, people are seeking human contact, connection, and unity. Whilst the globe has been going through a pandemic, much separation and heartache was caused, and many people have been yearning for love. A multitude of areas in people's lives has been affected, and both mental and physical health has been confronted. The world has had a shakeup and a loud calling message of a wake-up! It's through this new change that a mass re-evaluation has been had by many and for some, it's just too complex to deal with and will take some time to adjust. What can we do about this, how can we adapt and move forward and who can we become through this global paradigm shift? Well, as always, the change starts with us and then it spills over into other people, situations, circumstances, and causes an effect. It's important to connect within and love ourselves first and then we can demonstrate love and lead with love because we understand the value and power it has.

Every single person on the planet has the capability to be a leader, but it's our unique essence, inner value and style of leadership that will determine the message we portray and the potential impact it has on others. There are multiple styles of leadership, but no matter which style you consciously adopt; your inner narrative will subconsciously guide the way you lead. For example, if your narrative is fear-based, you become and demonstrate the fearful and fear-giving leader. If you're feeling confident, composed and at peace, then you become the caring and care-giving leader and you'll lead with love and in the long run, the latter will always thrive.

Fear and love are at the opposite ends of a psychological spectrum. Anyone with a fearful mindset tends to express pessimism and cynicism and this is then mirrored in their approach to leadership. The leader who leads from fear is more likely to assume their negative attitude and perception is shared by others. They often react rather than respond, project their own stress, uncertainty and pessimism through their words and actions and the tone of their voice is expressed from an unsettled place inside themselves. Overall, the fearful aura of the fearful leader is felt by all in their vicinity. It's not healthy or sustainable and in the long run, it all falls apart because it's a disempowering way of being, it has no life, it's anti-life and therefore cannot succeed and thrive.

Since the pandemic, a lot of confusion, uncertainty and fear has been portrayed through the media, government, and society and this has not been at all helpful for an individual's internal dialogue and emotional state, especially from a leadership perspective. However, can you imagine how the world would be if there was a pandemic of love? What effect would this have on humanity and the world? The vibration of the planet would rise and there would be an overspilling of loving energy creating healing, and harmony resulting in a state of joy, and all of this having emerged from an infectious love bug!

At the opposite end of the spectrum from leading with fear to leading with love, such as trust, kindness, compassion, vulnerability, courage, and empathy. When you lead from the heart, you lead from a place of engagement with purpose for something larger than yourself and take responsibility for your actions to nurture the potential of others and draw out their strengths. This approach opens the gateway to a trustworthy and authentic connection and ultimately fosters safety, creativity, productivity, and innovation. It's when we are at the service of others that we make a great difference and can cause a larger impact on many lives and the world by being a force for good and bringing about positive change, holding a space for other people's greatness, and consciously acting for the hive, not just the bee!

There is one energy, one power that we are all connected to in life here on earth. When we express our communication and emotions consciously and unconsciously, these are fuelled by the level of energy we expend, and this is the power that we release about them. The same applies through the application of focus and attention towards a person, situation, object, or imagination, depending on the depth of meaning and degree of attention we give, this will determine the amount of power that is released. To sum it up, we are walking energy source power beings, pulsing, and vibrating at a frequency that is generated from our Inner world through the mind, body and emotions and operating from our default setting on autopilot. Just like a chameleon, our energy changes according to our dominant thoughts and feelings that are expressed in our aetheric field, however, through self-awareness we each have the capacity to shift our internal state by focusing our attention, reprogramming the mind, and releasing stagnant energy to transform our experience of reality.

By adopting this level of awareness and allowing the power of love to be the tour guide through our actions and relationships in everything we do, this opens a whole new level of insight, connection, trust, and possibility. Whatever our gender is, there is an underlying recognition of energy to energy and a natural surrender that unfolds through the presence and power of love. However, more often from a female perspective, the emotional intelligence and wisdom of women is openly expressed through nurture, empathy, and intuition. Therefore, here lies an opportunity for women leading in our new world to harness the grace of this gift and let this force be the leader, the light in action, the way, and a win win for all.

A woman's nurturing instinct is part of her makeup which goes in her favour and in the realm of leadership. For many women, this quality comes naturally, but for others, it may not be so easy to express this way of being and this will depend on your life experience. Whether you are a mother or daughter and whatever your role is amidst your journey of womanhood, it's through the application and demonstration of conscious leadership and accountability from a loving perspective that this automatically creates space for psychological safety and belonging.

It's time for us to understand ourselves now more than ever, in the language of power and the language of love to the extent that we recognise that these are the forces of creation in themselves and that we must start thinking in terms of co-creation with the universal laws and how every single choice we make is an act of power. Power is the fundamental ingredient of the human experience and how we use it is paramount to what we are creating individually and collectively.

Love in its purest power has performed miracles, the substance that Jesus used was love, he was a master love teacher who channelled a high potent grace and healed thousands of people. Mahatma Gandhi was one of the most inspiring revolutionaries of the 20th century, he said, "love is the strongest force the world processes and yet it is the humblest imaginable." Mother Teresa made a profound difference to humanity through her devotion and compassion and universal love became one of the core principles of her legacy. The Dali Lama said, "the change in the world will be led by the woman of the west." Princess Diana's enduring legacy is one built upon the values of generosity, kindness and love which has long captivated the world and the inspiring poetic wisdom from Maya Angelo has touched many lives, she said "Love recognizes no barriers. It jumps hurdles, leaps over fences and penetrates walls to arrive at its destination full of hope."

Wherever you are on the Richter scale of expressing and leading with love, you can turn up the dial to increase your awareness and enhance your connection through the following approach. Think of yourself as a portal of love and a vessel of power, imagine your heart opening and see the lifeforce extending out from you and flowing into the people and environment around you. Cultivate the transforming qualities forementioned under the umbrella of love and give your full attention to another person by engaging in a state of pure presence to be able to really see the potential of another. It's through this level of consciousness, that the underlying energy flows from one person to another igniting the flame of humanity and allowing your creativity to open and flower into a state of heart coherence. Then from this potential space, we each can thrive and shine and express our true essence and unique talents and reciprocally everyone benefits from knowing that we have enriched and empowered the spirit of another. After all, we are all connected and equal parts of the same substance that permeates life, so why not become the embodiment of love, and lead wholeheartedly embracing our true nature living in a new dimension upon sacred mother earth.

About Tania Adams

Tania has a strong background with 30 years of frontline communications, sales and leadership skills within the corporate, retail and media sector. Her journey working as a coach began 18 years ago  and she specialises in the area of mindset and performance. A running theme of expression from Tania's client testimonials is about their profound transformation and frequently she receives feedback on how their lives have radically changed for the better.

Tania is passionate about the power of human potential and has an in-depth understanding of human behaviour; how the mind is conditioned for either success or failure. Her professional experience over an 18-year period has spanned three continents working with some of the biggest companies in the world including; Walmart, Tesco, Credit Suisse, BBC, Vodaphone and Calvin Klein. Tania has gained invaluable experience in her field throughout her journey as a coach.

Contact Tania at www.TaniaAdams.co.uk

MY MALU - A SPIRITUAL JOURNEY

By Sulu Nanai

A 'Malu' is a Samoan tattoo of cultural significance traditionally reserved for women, and means shelter and protection. It is applied from just below the knees to the upper thighs using traditional ink and markings and symbolises the story, the journey, and the heritage of the wearer.

As the years go by, I reflect on my life's journey thus far, focusing upon important events and lessons learned that have shaped me into becoming the woman I am today.

Strong and fiercely independent, I am a woman whose purpose is to be the best version of myself mentally, physically, and spiritually. To lead a positive and fulfilling life, including supporting my daughters, partner, family, and people in need. Discovering my purpose in life came about when I experienced great loss and immense grief. At that time, I questioned many things, and like sands in the hourglass, so began my healing journey and spiritual transformation leading to my 'Malu'.

The event that shaped me significantly and ultimately created the paradigm shift in my mindset occurred on the 4th March 2016. Forever etched in my memory, this impactful day was when my father passed away. It was the day that I experienced a spiritual awakening and an out-of-body phenomenon. I vividly remember my entire body trembling as I looked at my father lying on the bed with my mum standing at the head of the bed, holding his hand. He had a single teardrop running down the left side of his face and was facing me as I stood at the end of his bed. Feeling my heartbeat pound fiercely with intense stabbing pain, I watched my father take his last breath and his life disappear before my eyes. And with his last breath, I collapsed on the floor, and everything became a blur.

My mind and spirit temporarily left my body due to the absolute shock of losing the most important man in my life. It lasted only a few moments, but it changed me profoundly. It was most certainly the catalyst and the beginning of my spiritual and cultural transformation.

I understood my purpose from a cultural perspective during my father's last few months in palliative care. We spent many precious hours together talking about life in general, his life, his family, and 'Fa'asamoa' (Samoan culture and traditions). Although raised with Samoan culture and values, I was not entirely immersed in the Fa'asamoa way of life. In hindsight, I was pretty removed from it all.

So, when my father spoke to us of his wish for a traditional Samoan funeral, we fulfilled his wish with minimal knowledge and traditional understanding of what this truly meant. I recognise now that it was dad's parting gift for his children to learn and understand this facet of 'Fa'asamoa'.

We honoured my father's wish with a cultural farewell and celebration of his life that he would be proud of. Living the cultural practice leading up to, during, and after the funeral was enlightening and gave me a genuine appreciation of my Samoan culture and identity's importance.

They say time heals the pain, which is undoubtedly essential in my healing. In moments of reflection, the negative emotions of anger, sadness, and hurt are no more. I attribute this to many things, including faith, forgiveness, letting go, belief, and embarking on the journey of receiving my 'Malu'.

"And when great souls die, after a period peace blooms, slowly and always irregularly. Spaces fill with a kind of soothing electric vibration, Our senses, restored, never to be the same, whisper to us. They existed. We can be. Be and be better.
For they existed. "

— *Maya Angelou*

Life slowly returned to normalcy. I returned to

outrigger paddling and immersed myself in training with renewed vigour for the Queen Liliuokalani outrigger race, an international outrigger race event held on the Island of Kona, Hawaii.

We arrived at the Island of Kona in September 2016, and upon arrival, I instantly felt the 'mana' (spiritual essence and power) of the Island. There was a sense of belonging, and I felt the presence of my father and ancestors alike. I also knew intrinsically that my mind and heart's spiritual healing would begin on this magical Island.

On the day of the 18-mile outrigger canoe race (from one side of the Island to the other), our women's crew said a prayer then departed in our canoe to the start line. Whilst waiting at the start line with hundreds of paddlers from different parts of the world, I still strongly felt the mana of the Island assuring me of safety and protection on the water. It was a long and gruelling race that challenged me relentlessly, both mentally and physically. During the race, I felt my father's spirit with me, encouraging me to keep moving forward and fuelling my determination to be strong and push hard to the end. It was an emotional paddle, and at times I paddled with tears streaming down my face, speaking to my dad and letting him know how much I loved and missed him. After two hours of paddling, I felt my arms and body aching, and I asked my dad to give me further strength. I had to dig deep within myself to continue and continue. It was a massive race for the 'Flying Wahine2' women's team. We completed the race in two hours and thirty-nine minutes.

That experience was not only spiritual but also cathartic, a precursor to the spiritual journey that followed—my Malu.

"Strength does not come from physical capacity; it comes from an indomitable will"

— Mahatma Ghandi

A woman with a 'Malu' in the Samoan culture is a protector and shelter of her children, family and community. It is a sacred rite and hence has the importance of receiving support and blessings from the immediate family, extended family and ancestors alike. In November 2018, I was blessed and gifted my 'Malu' the marks of my identity, culture, family and ancestors.

The decision to receive my 'Malu' using the traditional tools that our ancestors used to receive theirs was a decision I did not take lightly. I researched and asked many questions seeking spiritual guidance from my father and ancestors: my immediate and extended family.

I ensured both my family and myself were well

prepared, following the customs, procedures, and taboos leading up to the day and on the day. We adhered to the strict Samoan protocols of receiving a malu extending to the final stage, the 'samaga' (blessing ceremony).

The day finally arrived, with my mind, body and spirit ready to receive my malu. I had an immediate spiritual connection with the 'Tufuga' (Master Tattooist) Su'a Peter Sulu'ape. His two assistants were referred to as the 'au solo' meaning 'wipe' whose role was to assist with wiping the excess ink and blood off my skin, ensuring my skin was always taut and clean.

My partner, mother, sisters, and daughters were all present, providing love, support and words of encouragement while sitting through the entire process with their legs covered by traditional Samoan 'fala' (fine mat). Lying face down on a fala, I prepared myself and was advised to relax and allow the process to guide me as it will. I surrendered to the process with faith and trust in Master Tattooist Su'a Peter Sulu'ape to gift me the markings of my family and cultural identity through spiritual guidance.

The tattooing started on the back of my left leg behind my knee; the Tufuga began with the rhythm of tap, tap...tap, tap, tap. Initially, the pain was tolerable; however, the pain intensified as time went on. The tapping tempo became quicker and longer between 'solo' breaks, and I found myself searching deep within for strength. I felt my father's presence throughout the process, giving me power. As the pain intensified with each tapping of ink markings, I started thinking about the pain my maternal grandmother endured for her malu. I also thought about the pain my paternal grandfather suffered from his 'tatau' (a Samoan tattoo traditionally reserved for men), and at the height of the pain, I had a vision of my grandfather.

He majestically stood over me, our family 'Matai' (Samoan High Chief), in traditional Samoan chief attire for a formal event or ceremony. His presence, along with my dad's spirit, armed me with the courage to bear the pain. Deep within my heart and soul, I felt that their presence was a sign of acceptance and was the defining moment in completing my Malu.

It took two hours and fifteen minutes to complete my Malu, and in all that time, I was surrounded by my loved ones feeling their joy, pride, and encouragement. Gratitude, peace, and spiritual love embraced me. I felt excited with a renewed sense of purpose.

I knew it was the beginning of another leg of my

journey as a leader, protector and shelter for my family and in service of those in need. A journey of embracing the past, the present, and the future with gratitude and an ultim8 mindset.

"Every day, wake up with gratitude and a positive mindset, and you will achieve goals and desired outcomes." — Ultim8 Mindset, be the best version of you.

About Sulu Nanai

Sulu lives in Melbourne, Australia. She is an accomplished IT professional with 20+ years of experience in leadership roles across various organisations in the public and private sectors.

Sulu is also a qualified Master NLP Practitioner and Coach, Master NLP Time Line Therapy® Coach, and Hypnotherapist.

Sulu is the founder and owner of 'Ultim8 Mindset' a coaching and mentoring business. As a Life and Leadership Coach, she specialises in breakthrough sessions with clients enabling them to achieve their desired outcomes and goals aligned to personal growth, career, health/wellness, and relationships.

She is passionate about working with her clients, elevating them to become the best version of themselves by understanding their thought patterns, language, and behavioural habits. Her work enables clients to release their blockages by clearing negative emotions and limiting beliefs.

Sulu believes in offering her clients a personalised approach to achieve their desired outcomes using several modalities and submodalities, including and not limited to NLP and Time Line Therapy®.

Connect with Sulu: www.ultim8mindset.com

THE ROAD TO IMPORTANCE

By Sarah Presley

"Who is the most important person to you?", asked the lady with the sparkly blue eyes. I began to list all the members of my family and as I did, I recalled a time when my Gran would encourage me to kneel by the side of my bed and pray to keep my family safe. As a child I would worry how I might miss someone off the prayer list, and the same flash of anxiety I felt back then, washed over me now. Mid-list, she stopped me, and said, "Why haven't you included yourself? Are you not important too?".

I stared blankly back at her, wondering if this was a trick question. Surely if I considered myself important, might I be judged as being conceited or selfish by everyone else in the room? I wasn't even sure I felt I was important, and anyway, I was here to learn about Reiki, not to process uncomfortable questions.

I had been diagnosed some years before with chronic fatigue and I was leaving no stone unturned in my quest to discover how to return to the optimum of health and wellbeing. The lady asking the questions was a Reiki Master and this was how I had found myself on her Reiki course, contemplating these questions. At this point, I had no way of knowing how this exchange would be a contributing factor to turning my life around, and going on to set up my own business supporting those going through a tough time. Or how it would continue to inspire me to take the next step to teach individuals who wanted to set up their own business supporting others.

Stopping life

Prior to my diagnosis, I was the epitome of the "work hard, play hard" lifestyle which was prominent in the 90s. As well as working my way up the career ladder for a corporate company, I was also pursuing my dreams of being a singer in a punk rock band. By the age of 26, my dreams were already coming to fruition: my band was touring the UK whilst being sponsored by a top London modelling agency and starting to gain record industry interest. On the outside I appeared happy and confident, but on the inside, I was living on a constant knife-edge of fear and anxiety. I worried continuously about not being liked and my need for approval meant I spent much of my energy trying to please everyone around me.

The relentless stressful situations I found myself in meant my body was locked into a fight or flight response, trapped in an ever-decreasing cycle, and I couldn't find the key to escape. Eventually, due to the sheer exhaustion I felt on a daily basis, I had to stop working and singing in the band - in fact I had to stop my entire life - and I watched my dreams fall apart, wondering where it had all gone wrong.

The road to diagnosis of chronic fatigue was long, and I felt I had been given a life sentence of misery. In addition to the fatigue symptoms, I also suffered with anxiety and depression and it was easy to slip into losing the point of life. But my determination to be well again was stronger and I decided to seek out ways to wellness by reading self-help books and attending various complementary therapy sessions and courses, which is how I found myself attending the Reiki One course.

My response to being asked if I considered myself to be important was to say "No". My self-esteem was at an all-time low and I considered myself at the bottom of the pile. My Reiki Master suggested that by burning out I had put the needs of everyone else before my own, and perhaps there was another way, a way in which I would consider my own needs as important as everyone around me.

As this realisation sank in, I could feel a change within me. I realised it was time to treat myself as I would my own best friend.

The Golden Rule
The Golden Rule, the principle of treating others as one would like to be treated, features in many

religions and cultures. It has been ingrained into our psyche. Giving to others is a heart centred approach however, we may judge ourselves harshly for giving the same regard and care to the self, considering it of a selfish nature. Whilst contemplating the needs of others is a kind and thoughtful act, when it comes to the detriment of your health and wellbeing then the balance needs to be addressed.

Of course, I didn't know this when the question of my own importance was put to me, I simply knew the question had struck a chord and realised it was time to do something different. As the old adage says, "If you always do what you've always done, you'll always get what you've always got", so for me, it was time to make some changes. I began to understand how my time, effort and energy are precious, and how it was now time to use it wisely. I also identified how often life, and the people around me, were creating a mirror. If I was unable to respect my time then the people around me would find it hard to respect my time too.

Giving and Receiving

Our physical heart receives deoxygenated blood from the right side, it then pumps the blood to the lungs where it picks up a fresh supply of oxygen before returning to the left side of the heart to be pumped around the body. So, our physical heart's function is to give and receive.

If we apply this to our emotional heart, we will realise we need to have the same balance. We will see we need to give to ourselves, to receive, so that we can continue to give to others.

I realised how I needed to take a personal responsibility for my own healing and so I began a daily meditation practice as well as supporting myself with reiki self-healing treatments. I began to enjoy the process of giving to myself as I could see a direct link between this and being able to enjoy great health. I realised I was honouring and respecting myself for the first time in my life and this helped me to set positive boundaries.

Self-care

Following my recovery from chronic fatigue, I felt a desire to share what I had learnt along the way and so I set up my own holistic therapy business. Over the years it has been a joy to witness my clients stepping on their own road to importance. However, I also realised how creating the right professional boundaries to my business was imperative, and so I developed a set of principles through which I continued to honour my energy and time.

Now, training Meditation Teachers and Reiki Practitioners, I encourage students to create their own positive boundaries too, as they will discover how supporting others involves a lot of giving. Also, running a business requires personal resilience. To have the drive to do what needs to be done, looking after and considering the self is key. Prioritising the self isn't selfish, it's understanding the bigger picture of your life.

Some find a reluctance in self-care as it is easy for the word "self" to immediately be associated with the word "selfish". Taking the "ish" part of the word, we can see a correlation with the Sanskrit word "Isht" which translates as beloved or respected. So, in effect, if we are self-ish, we are respecting and seeing ourselves as beloved beings!

The road to importance is doing what is necessary to create a balance to life, and this is the balance of giving and receiving to yourself. It may involve making space in your day for meditation or exercise. Or it may be how you nurture and fuel your body with food. It could be carving out time to read a good book. Or knowing it's ok to say "no" when necessary. It can also come by saying "yes" and accepting help from others. Or from knowing you don't always have to go it alone.

It is also about seeing yourself as your own best friend, someone who truly deserves the regard and care as much as everyone else. Someone who is willing to treat the self with kindness and compassion. It is understanding how your time and your energy are precious and how it should be nurtured, contained and honoured.

So, who is the most important person to you right now and how can you take steps to ensure you are on the list?

About Sarah Presley

From Punk to Meditation Teacher, with a detour with Chronic Fatigue in between.

Sarah Presley's life has been full of twists and turns, and ups and downs. Through this she has developed a tool-kit of wellness techniques which she has shared in her holistic business for almost 20 years, in a quest to support others going through a tough time.

Utilising everything she learnt along the way, Sarah now trains Meditation Teachers and Reiki Practitioners, to create a successful business to they can bring their life changing skills to their corner of the world.

www.sarahpresley.co.uk

www.facebook.com/sarahpresleymeditation

www.instagram.com/sarahpresleymeditation

LEADING FROM WITHIN

By Caroline Durham

The junior high school gymnasium rumbled with the noise of 800+ students crammed onto wooden bleachers and chairs covering the basketball court. The principal called for quiet, asking that everyone listen to the speeches about to be given. The smell of countless gym classes and basketball games made the air stale. Seated under one of the baskets at the far end of the gym, along with all the other candidates running for student government office, I ran my speech through my head, "I'm Caroline Durham and I am running for student government reporter."

The role of reporter was much like that of a committee secretary. I chose a support position to be engaged in rather than a higher office like president. In this role, I would have more connection with the student body, and be responsible for sharing out the student leadership's decisions. I wanted a position that led to connection with my classmates.

Leadership comes from all places and in many forms.

Being a leader is something that always came natural to me. 'Natural' meaning I didn't say 'I'm going to be a leader', I just followed my heart, my desires and passions, and they flowed into leadership roles. Sometimes, without even realising how it happened, I've ended up at the helm.

Now in my mid-50s, I realise that it is the internal that drives me to be a leader. The Divine within that drives my leadership and feeds the fuel of leading others to be leaders.

The Divine is within each one of us. Sit with that. The Divine is within you. And it is the Divine that steers us to lead. It was the Divine Spirit that I, unknowingly, was connected to that day, in the school gymnasium.

The Divine was not always obvious to me. I spent years meandering through many spiritual paths of my life – raised in the Southern Baptist Church, exploring Catholicism in my 30s, engaging in no spiritual practice for many years starting in college – I became aware that all those years I was seeking a higher power outside of me., Yet, God who created this Universe, has been inside me all along. Heart, soul, Spirit, our inner being, even with the meandering, I was always connected to my heart.

It was years of being weighed down by my work as a public defender that led me to the depth of spiritual practice that has allowed me to flourish as a leader. Even with my spiritual meanderings, my passion for people, for connection, for seeing people succeed, has been a constant underpinning in my work.

For almost thirty years, I served as a public defender – representing people charged with crimes, fighting for their freedom, fighting for justice, fighting for their stories to be heard. From the early years of my career, representing people charged with the most egregious crimes (murder, assault, serious drug offenses) was my specialty.

With every person I have met in my work, I have seen leadership qualities. Alongside the positive, I have observed the crushing impact of racist systems, poverty, poor education support and health concerns that too often left my clients with having only bad choices from which to choose.

The deep impact of second-hand trauma in their life stories as I fought for their freedom, got to know their families, and dealt with their crimes wore me down. While I pushed on from court hearing, to trial, to jail visits, my body and soul were taking a beating. Amid the professional turmoil that was my work, I began to notice more and more, the calm of two very dear friends.

For more than a decade, Shelly and Stacey had been engaged in deep Buddhist practices and studies. Meditation was daily for them. All I knew was I wanted some of the calm and grace that flowed from them. I engaged them in conversations and I began to go to the meditation centre with them. The teachings and the practices fed my soul and my knowledge like oxygen for a newborn baby. By simply living their truth, Shelly and Stacey were leading by being grounded. Through that quiet leadership, they empowered me to be stronger.

It was through this deepening connection to the Divine Spirit that I became more intentional and fully aware of the countless ways I am a leader. Knowing that I am of Divine nature and that every person is of Divine nature, allows me to see myself fully. Seeing the fullness, richness and beauty that is in each and every person on this Earth, I understand my responsibility to serve goodness. Only in knowing that Divine Spirit flows through me did I fully understand my purpose and strength as a leader.

My spiritual practices in Buddhism and New Thought teachings shined the light most brightly on this knowing. The great awareness maker is breath and meditation. Meditation allows us to release the busyness of mind that can distract us from outer-doing. One thought leading to the next creating too often stress of tasks undone. Meditation takes us to a place of releasing attachment to thoughts, to the constant running and doing that life brings.

As you read this, I ask you to pause. Take a deep breath in. Hold that breath for a second or two before exhaling. Feel the chair or floor or ground beneath you at this moment. Breath in again. Grounding in oneself allows a knowing of self, a knowing of calm, a knowing of limitlessness.

Why is meditation an important strength as a leader? When I am weighed down by the everyday, I lose track of the greater vision that I am here to serve. Taking time in meditation, in spiritual practice, creates internal spaciousness that allows me to hear the Divine speak of my role as a leader.

During that morning assembly back in junior high school, I stepped up to the microphone in front of all my classmates, a bit nervous – though I'd spent countless hours in front of the bathroom mirror practising my speech. "Bringing you thoughtfulness and …..", my mind went blank. The words on the index cards, left at home as I didn't think I needed them, no longer streaming like a teletype in my brain. I sat down, unable to finish calling these 7th and 8th graders to action to elect me, so I could serve them. I returned to my chair. The auditorium was silent.

Being a leader simply means having the fortitude to step up in your truth, to dig deep, sometimes for the courage to say what needs to be said, to take action. And so, I dug deep that morning in 7th grade. While others gave their speeches, I dug deep in the recesses of my mind for the words. I found my breath and focus. And when given a second opportunity, I stood before my classmates and called for their support.

As I finished, the auditorium was no longer silent. It was filled with the noise of all those 12 and 13-year-olds, on their feet, shouting in awe as I hadn't hidden away in the midst of my earlier foible. To stand up tall, speak clearly and share my truth, after completely stumbling before, showed them how to do the same. I stepped into leadership that day.

And so I implore each of you to go deep within yourselves in those moments of discomfort. That is when the Divine speaks to you. Stand in your truth. Speak your words. Be the leader within and you will inevitably be a leader for others too.

About Caroline Durham

Caroline Durham, a queer woman born and raised in New Orleans, Louisiana, is a social justice activist, abolitionist, wellness coach and empowerment speaker. Serving as founding Executive Director for the St. Charles Center for
Faith + Action, she believes in the power each individual carry within them. With thirty-plus years of justice advocacy, she's fought for the freedom of hundreds individuals charged with crimes in state and federal court.

Through her previous role as Legal and Policy Director for Georgia Appleseed Center for Law and Justice, she worked tirelessly to push forward policy to dismantle the school to prison pipeline and to bring healthy housing to families across Georgia. She has extensive experience training advocates on how to effectively navigate criminal courts, provide client-centered services, and bring about systemic change through case-by-case work.

A graduate of the Barbara King School of Ministry and Tulane Law School, she understands the interwoven role of divine calling as powerful changemaking. Caroline has served as a member of several boards and volunteered with community organizations, including African American Family Services and the Veterans Defense Project. Contact Caroline at cdurham@stcharlesave.center

WHY KNOWING YOURSELF IS THE BEST PLACE TO START

By Tracey Miller

I knew I was capable of a lot more than I was being. There was something innate that I couldn't put my finger on. I wanted to lead, be inspiring, show the way. But how are you meant to do that for others when you can't even inspire yourself?

As a teenager, I was very self-conscious and withdrawn. At 16, I secured a three-week work experience placement in the graphic design department at the British Standards Institution. I had zero confidence and I was so awkward. Every day it was a challenge just to show up and be present. There was another girl there, the same age, who was confident, outspoken and having a vastly different experience to me. I watched her every day, comparing her attitude, mannerisms and interactions with others until, one day, I decided to be different. I was going to be confident too.

Obviously, instead of just imitating her natural confidence, or finding my own true self, my new persona was more of a train wreck of over-confidence compensating for excruciatingly low self-esteem. Loud and inappropriate comments, lots of blushing, a vast amount of hiding my true self and a good dose of standoffish bitch to cover any of the gaps. Nailed it!

In all honesty, this strategy yielded vastly improved results from where I'd been, so I stuck with it, cultivating and honing this persona. I went on to take a business degree, choosing the psychology option which delved into personality testing. I fell in love with these questionnaires that would pop out answers about who you were. I found solace in them as an explanation, or perhaps a justification, of why I was who I was. I always came out as a rowdy extrovert and I liked that. I leaned into it and purposefully cultivated that persona to give me the sense of identity I so desperately desired.

I took this persona into IT sales where it worked brilliantly for 15 years, on the outside, at least. The problem was that it wasn't the true me. It was exhausting keeping up the front and I suffered mercilessly from imposter syndrome, believing every day that I would be found out for the fraud I was. The anxiety was real and the constant noise in my head of my own self-denigrating thoughts was overwhelming. I sought solace in drink, recreational drugs, and anything else that would temporarily ease the turmoil. Obviously not a permanent solution and I knew I needed to find one.

I've always been interested in knowing who I am. I think it stemmed from being adopted and feeling like I never really fitted into my family, or anywhere for that matter. I struggled a lot with my sense of identity. I was definitely different. Still am, actually. Even today, as I head into my fifties, my views are completely at odds with my family.

I was terrified of getting to know myself more. I had an inherent inability to have a properly connected intimate relationship. I knew I had 'issues', childhood experiences saw to that, but even when I was on my best behaviour, things just kept falling apart and patterns would repeat themselves. My biggest fear was that if I went there, I might find out I was actually a total loser, an imposter, unworthy of love. At least, whilst I didn't know there was some hope.

I embarked on the journey to really discover who I am about 15 years ago. Like many women I talk to, a significant event creates the catalyst for change and in my case it was a shitty divorce. I lost everything – my dream house, my job, my security, my future – it all came crashing down and I had to start again. I tried hard to regain my footing in the old life of IT sales, fast cars, plenty of cash and unhealthy relationships, but I was flogging a dead horse. That life was over and I knew it every day I woke up to go to work.

I am infinitely grateful for that time now, though. It was the catalyst for me finding true love, finding real purpose in my work and finding myself. I'd love to say I shifted elegantly from one life to the other, but that would be a lie. It involved massive amounts of confusion and chaos, loads of snot and tears, feeling lost and like I'd fallen into an abyss on multiple occasions, screaming and shouting, abject terror, immense anxiety and a desire to 'get off' almost every day.

But it was worth it.

I believe that getting to know yourself, really know yourself, is one of the greatest adventures of our time on this planet. Knowing yourself takes a journey of deep understanding. It doesn't stop with a skim over the surface about what your favourite food is, or where your g-spots are, although this isn't a bad place to start. It's pushing past all the surface stuff and going deep below, into the depths of your soul, to find out what lies beneath the armour, the personas, the cultivated behaviour patterns, the survival strategies, the bits we love and the bits we loathe.

It takes immense courage to keep peeling back the layers, despite not knowing what lies beneath. Once you start on the journey there is no going back. (Well, there is, but it generally looks like a tragic mid-life crisis and it's really only a temporary pause in proceedings, so best avoided all round.)

The journey to knowing yourself is arduous. The hardest part is the cyclical nature of confusion and enlightenment. You literally go from the darkest depths of despair to everything suddenly making sense, back to more bloody darkness, and so on. It's exhausting! But you eventually realise that 'this too shall pass' and every time you cycle you evolve just a little bit more. With practice, you learn to embrace the dark times, leaning into them rather than fighting them.

I believe the biggest challenges on our path towards understanding the truth about ourselves are two-fold. First, we try to rationalise it and make sense of it with logic. And second, we try to control the process, avoid confusion and uncertainty.

We have been conditioned over many years to believe that intuition has no value without backed up facts and figures. I have this debate often. The incessant 'follow the science' mantra that's being hammered home on every mainstream media outlet right now is a perfect example of this. When did questioning things become obsolete? What about plain old common sense? Any woman who has ever had the hairs on the back of her neck rise up in warning, or been compelled to contact someone randomly only to find out they needed you in that moment, or turned just as their child is about to hurt themselves, knows that our innate intuition and wisdom has more power than we can possibly fathom.

Once we come back to our true intuitive nature, wisdom shows us that these deep processes are not logical, or certainly not in the way our human brain understands logic. Once we relax into and trust our intuition and the innate wisdom we are all born with, we can let go of the need to control every part of the process and trust. Whilst this doesn't alleviate all the pain, pain being part of the process, it does make the whole journey a whole lot more pleasurable and enables us to embrace each cycle with more grace.

So why would we attempt this terrifying, arduous journey of self-discovery? One, because I think we're coming to a time when we're going to have to, so it's worth getting a head start. And two, because without it we are only experiencing a fraction of what is possible for us.

In case you hadn't noticed, this planet is going through some pretty radical changes. We are witnessing unbelievable shifts, the dismantling of systems that no longer work for us. There are dramatic changes to our way of life, our economies, our technological and political landscapes, our energy and our humanity. We are being challenged, 'squeezed', and our shit is rising to the surface. This is a gift as it shortcuts a lot of the work in finding the hidden stuff, but it's incredibly uncomfortable and many people are fighting it.

I learned the term 'cognitive dissonance' recently. When we receive conflicting information that challenges our very core beliefs, the discomfort becomes too much to bear and we rationalise, ignore and even deny anything that doesn't fit with our core belief. This makes sense; we want to feel safe. It's built into our DNA, so embarking on a journey that is filled with unknowing, trepidation, chaos and confusion goes against our basic survival instincts - but it's also exciting, mysterious, and full of awe and wonder. At some point this experience is going to end, and I for one want to look back and know I gave it my all.

And the rewards? Well, how about; complete confidence in who you are, being able to give and receive unconditional love, setting and maintaining clear boundaries, living predominantly in joy, regardless of what goes on around you, being fully present in the moment, being able to be of deeper service to others, having the courage to be disliked and making fewer apologies.

I'll take those, thank you very much.

So where to start? Start with an intention. Be clear in your mind and announce that you wish to embark on the journey of self-discovery. Trust your intuition and innate wisdom. Listen to your heart. You'll be amazed at what opens up to you and what learning experiences become available.

I still love personality tests. A particular favourite of mine is The Vitality Test by Nicholas Haines, but I also like Talent Dynamics. Work on your confidence and self-esteem as you embark on this journey, too. I recommend The 28-Day Self-Esteem Reboot Challenge by George Swift. I also loved The Untethered Soul by Michael Singer, the Empath's Survival Guide by Judith Orloff and Attached by Amir Levine and Rachel Heller.

When you embark on this journey, don't just look for validation of what you already believe to be true. Be open to what comes up. And beware of labels. They can be really helpful but they can also put you in a box and we are often way more complex than that.

Over the last 15 years I've found out that;

I have General Anxiety Disorder,

I am anxious-avoidant in relationships (only 4% of people are this type and it's the hardest to work with),

I am Wood energy, which is vibrant and exciting and also very controlling when stressed, which I am a lot because I have General Anxiety Disorder,

I'm an empath, which means I can feel other people's emotions and often misinterpret them in close relationships, which makes me stressed, which makes me controlling because I'm a Wood energy, which isn't great for intimate relationships.

This understanding has been revolutionary for me. I've been able to share these findings with my intimate partner and grow with him as he develops and grows in our relationship. It means I am so much kinder to myself, handling my flaws and failings with significantly more compassion, and I'm developing a deep and unconditional love for myself and for my fellow humans, something that touches this life with magic.

I am very much a work in progress but I am enjoying the process and leaning into the tough times as part of the experience.

You have everything you need within you to cultivate the life you want and the experience you want to have. Have the courage to peel back those layers, be brave. I promise you, if you keep going, you will love what you find. I love you already.

About Tracey Miller

Tracey Miller is a professional coach, mentor, facilitator, empath and healer. She's worked with hundreds of small businesses over 10 years helping them generate more income, create more freedom and build the business they want.

The last 12 months has seen unprecedented changes in our economic, political, technological and social landscapes. Whilst it's been a challenging rollercoaster for small business owners, there is so much potential out there and she's on a mission to help people tap into it.

Contact Tracey at
tracey.miller@biggerbrighterbolder.co.uk.

THE DIVINE FEMININE LEADS

By Teresa Corso

As I write this chapter, I am in the Heart of the Great Barrier Reef, on a beautiful beach on the Whitsundays. An area surrounded by 74 tropical islands, in a majestic part of Australia. I am soaking up the rays in admiration and wonder of all that is before me.

I have just spent 4 extraordinary days with my daughter, a young woman who is reflecting on life, choices, friendships, on surrendering to the unknown and navigating uncharted waters.

Over these last few days I have been contemplating on the importance of Grandmothers, Mothers, Aunties, Sisters, and girlfriends – WOMEN, sharing stories, passing on knowledge and teachings with other younger women. There is something quite sacred in sharing our life lessons. It is a gift, a legacy and a right-of-passage. Planting seeds of wisdom and nurturing these with love for growth, for courageous adventures and extraordinary leadership. This is our fragrance, our scent, that lingers well beyond our earthly existence.

Unfortunately, both my grandmothers transitioned long before I entered the world. For many years I longed for the embrace of "unconditional grandmotherly love". Many of my friends had a grandmother or an elder that shared with them ancient secrets, traditional ways and family recipes. Many heard stories that were passed on through generations, spent time in nature, observing the universal laws and their relationship to the elements. Some learnt a craft such as knitting or weaving and metaphorically had the opportunity to understand the true workings of the universe; the role of interconnection and purpose, in weaving one's unique fabric of life. It is for all these reasons I yearned for the presence of the "Crone" archetype. That WISE one.

My life, however, was incredibly blessed. I was raised by loving parents. My mother, mystical, beautiful and youthful, was compassionate, loving and incredibly intuitive and whose spiritual understanding was beyond the confines of religious dogmas. I hold her in high esteem.

As a child I became aware of the distinction between masculine and feminine energy, at the time I only saw this as linear, in physical form in my family. Traditional values and roles passed on through culture and community. This often left me questioning my purpose and wondering how I could flow beyond the perceived limitations or boundaries in my life?

For many years I danced between the two energies. Leaning towards the more dominant masculine energy. I saw success, strength and stamina as masculine traits and aspired to attain these. I was proud of my physical and emotional capacities. It was only when I became pregnant that something within, changed. A softness was emerging. A strong and determined softness. Somehow a vortex opened allowing the Goddess/feminine within to whisper, weave and create my new path. I embraced the Womb(an) energy that was emerging.

So, I left the stability of the corporate world to enter a field that spoke to my inner soul. I was given many insights through visions, dreams, so called coincidences and chance meetings. The signs were clear. It was time to venture out on a new course, my soul's path. This "gamble" gifted me a sacred blessing, in the form of a Hawaiian Elder and Kumu (teacher) and whom I call my soul's doula, one who would be my companion on journeying into self-inquisition, understanding purpose and Loving in Action.

As I continue to write, the waves are breaking on the shoreline, I feel nurtured by my first mother and blessed for all that she provides. For the gift of breath, observation, and abundance. I am also grateful for the love and inspiration I receive from the three above mentioned women. My Daughter, my Mother and my Kumu. Incredible and unique women who challenge and encourage me. Whose love ignites my inner spirit and urges her (my spirit) to soar. A love that inspires me to lead with a courageous Heart.

But how does one lead with a courageous heart? Courage is a word that has evolved over time, some may interpret it as "bravery" others as "inner strength". The root word of courage is "cor" derived from the Latin word heart, so to lead with a courageous heart could be interpreted as to speak your truth from the heart. To know and understand your values and principles. Feeling grounded in who you are and taking actions that align with your heart's blueprint. To lead courageously honours your authentic self and your soul's purpose.

To lead with a courageous heart is to tap into a well spring deep within your core.

Over time I realised that the well spring is where Spirit exists within me. It is here that I feel intuitively guided by the compass of my soul. It is the dwelling place of infinite intelligence. So, I surrendered and finally trusted the voice deep within. A voice I refer to as the Divine Goddess or the Divine Feminine, and I allow her to rise into my mind, body and soul. The Goddess within me is an energy, my energy, my connection to Source, to infinite love.

The divine feminine rising is not a movement, nor a riot, it is a consciousness. An awakening.

Understanding that both the masculine and feminine energies exist in each of us. Balancing the "doing" and "hunting" (masculine) energy with the 'receiving' and 'creating' (feminine) energy and understanding that they are not siloed but co-exist in each of us. It is looking deeper at the relationship of the yin/yang, the harmony, flow and balance that is created between the positive and the negative. It is examining the relationship of the sun and moon and noticing how essential and interconnected the two are to our planet.

The divine feminine rising celebrates the lifecycle of all things. It is fertility, creation, and birthing of new ideas, concepts and behaviours. It is a leadership style with a foundation based on honouring, understanding and celebrating each other. It explores all ideas, creates positive changes and makes decisions that combine intuition, heart, courage and acumen. Leadership that fosters growth, compassion and abundance on all levels.

I likened the Divine Feminine consciousness to that of the historical character Joan of Arc. One who represents power, courage, and steadfast determination. One who is strong in her understanding of self, is connected to infinite spirit and who trusts her intuition. One who leads courageously with the heart for the greater good of humanity.

Reflection:

Judge not her ways but love her unconditionally

In loving her you become the invincible power,

The unstoppable force that overcomes all obstacles

You develop an inner glow, a knowing and trust

And will ebb and flow through life with ease

Honour her, forgive her, cherish her,

Adorn her, love on her, reconnect with her and

Treasure the Goddess within you

Meditation:

Take 3 gentle breaths and become comfortable in your surroundings

Gently place one hand on your heart centre

The other hand on your abdomen (womb)

Take a moment to inhale and connect to your breath,

This sacred breath of life

Allow this breath to filter into your abdomen (womb)

(Breathe x3)

Affirm all or choose those that call out to you:
I AM Grace
I AM Compassion
I AM Courage
I AM Strength
I AM Understanding
I AM LOVE
I AM The Phoenix
I AM The Creator Within,
I AM The Goddess
I AM The Divine Feminine
I Create
I Flourish
I Teach
I Lead
I Rise

Embody the essence of these words by imagining a golden light touching the crown of your head and flowing all the way down through to your feet.

Allow this light to radiate out into your world, feel this loving energy expand further out into the universe

Ask: What is it I wish to create for myself, for others, for humanity?

Call it in

Ask: What message does my goddess have for me? Listen be still, hear her whisper

Write your message down for you to refer to again.

Give thanks for these insights and affirm:

I am the goddess

I honour you

And I am grateful to be re-acquainted with you, today.

Thank you, I love you.

About Teresa Corso

Teresa Corso refers to herself as a barefoot Earth adventurer and a lover of Life. She is an International Author, Speaker and Co-host of The Thread Wellbeing Podcast. Teresa is also the founding Director of Soulitude Massage and Wellness, a holistic wellbeing studio focusing on healing modalities such as Hawaiian healing and bodywork, Lomi Lomi, Oncology and remedial massage as well as different forms of energy healing.

She is Spiritual Coach, End of Life Doula, and Wayapa Wuurrk Meditation facilitiator and enjoys working in all realms of health and wellbeing. Having recently been ordained as a New Thought Minister Teresa is often referred to as Rev T, or more commonly Soul Sista T. Teresa runs a number of workshops and retreats both locally and internationally providing space for individuals to connect to their inner spirit and divinity. Her favourite quote is "LOVE is my lineage;

GRATITUDE is my religion" Meggan Watterson:
The Divine feminine oracle

Contact Teresa at soulitudemw@gmail.com

THE RIPPLE OF ROLE MODELS

By Gill McKay

I am a firm believer that leadership is about relationships – who we relate to and who we willingly want to follow.

It is of course context dependent. In distinct circumstances different people have built up trust, respect and alignment and through their impact have proven themselves worthy of following.

Simply put, they have acted as role models in how they show up every day. Role models are like pebbles, creating a ripple through their impact that echoes across the world, capturing others in the magic of their message.

Role models have always been of interest to me. From a young age, I recognised the amazingness of people and the ripple effect they have on others. My paternal grandmother lived with us. She was widowed when my father was seven and his younger brother five. She was forced to work in the 1930s and managed to raise her two boys to go to university. Dad became a doctor and my uncle an engineer.

Her abundance continued into her later years and my friends loved coming to our house to play games with her. She was simply known in our neighbourhood as "Granny". Her energy and magnetism caused ripples of friendship and love, constantly attracting people into her life to share her wisdom.

Without her knowing it, she gave me ambition and enabled a future conversation with myself about the sort of person and role model I wanted to be in the world. Thank you, Granny.

We Are All Role Models

One of the most enjoyable periods in my corporate life was running the Leadership School for the Unisys University in EMEA. It was where I discovered the benefits of using neuroscience as a tool for facilitating deeper conversations with learners and when I started to develop my thinking about the importance of role models in leadership.

I co-developed a leadership workshop and distinctly remember the impact of an exercise we ran entitled "Personal Best". It invited participants to think back to their life and work experiences where they believed they had shown their leadership skills, what they had brought to the situation and what they had learned from it.

As well as the experiences of project, team or sales leadership at work, it was inspiring to hear stories around the many different scenarios the exercise brought to mind. We learned of participants running scout teams, Saturday morning playgroups, keep-fit groups, children's football teams, pet therapy for the elderly, choirs, amateur dramatics societies to name a few.

Many different contexts but all with similar themes – leaders role modelling the way ahead with a vision to achieve something positive for others to enable them to grow from it, inspire them to learn and encourage them to take action and feel good about themselves. Universally a sense of community, abundance and growth underpinned all activities.

New Leadership For Now

The world has changed and I believe we need a new type of leadership built on values, love, compassion, empowerment and inclusion. One that embraces diversity, humility, integrity and vulnerability. One that offers conscious authentic role modelling.

Over the years a few themes of what great role models have in common, have emerged for me. Here are three of them:

1: they appreciate difference and respect others;

2: they operate with integrity and build trust from their values;

3: they consistently show up as the authentic, real person they are.

I believe lessons on diversity, alignment of values and authenticity form the basis for the ideal role model. Walking the talk and leading by example in this way is the new leadership we need today.

1: *Appreciate Difference*

I was born with a hole between the two ventricles in my heart. All those years ago, it was a huge worry to my parents, both doctors, especially as my elder sister had died young of a brain tumour. I was blissfully unaware of the mortality rate, but just knew I was different.

I was painfully thin with blue lips and nails and took regular time out of school for hospital visits. There was initially a fund to send me to a hospital in the US, then the relief of being accepted into the magnificent Great Ormond Street in London where I was the fifth operation of its type performed in the UK.

It was wonderful to be cured yet I remained on half day schooling for a year, with no PE – and I longed to fit in. No wonder I became an incredibly rebellious teenager!

But this start in life gave me a feel for the joy of individuality. I couldn't have asked for better role modelling as my parents encouraged me to blossom into whoever I chose to be, to be different from my brother and sister. We all respected each other, honoured our uniqueness yet worked so beautifully as a whole together, we were a closely knit family.

I know my upbringing has fuelled my desire to work with people to embrace the individuals they are. And to facilitate conversations around the richness of diversity and difference in teams and organisations. When people respect and appreciate one another's preferences and opinions, that is when the magic can happen. If we were all alike, sharing an identical perspective, then possibilities, new ideas and creativity would narrow down. What a robotic world that would be.

Throughout my 30 years of work, the leaders who were role models for me all valued difference and diversity, had abundant, growth mindsets and listened to everyone's views. They brought people together because of their difference, understanding that diversity brings with it new horizons. They knew that when people believe that their opinion counts, that their contribution matters and that they have a place at the table, it is a hugely empowering place to be.

2: *Know Your Values*

My coaching client Derek* in a global sales organisation was a successful country manager, yet felt he didn't have a voice. Our work together revealed he believed he wasn't extrovert enough, lacking the gravitas and presence to climb the leadership ladder.

There were many visible leaders in his company who were outstanding orators. Put them on a stage or in front of a camera and they would have any audience hooked with their stories, anecdotes and inspirational, world changing promises. But this just wasn't the man Derek was.

Derek was reflective, calm under pressure, compassionate and humble. His core values were around abundance, integrity, fairness, curiosity and compassion. He always operated from his values yet he didn't realise how clear that was to his team, his clients and all his stakeholders. He wasn't aware that he was a role model to them, that they would follow him to the end of the earth. That they believed in him with both their hearts and their heads.

Once he removed himself from the limiting belief of what he "should be", put a language to his values and the strengths that emanated from them, he gave himself permission to choose his career path.

Values matter. When you are congruent with your values there is no resistance. You will experience ease and flow in your life and your work without trying. You will role model consistent alignment to the world.

3: *Be The Authentic You*

Early on in my corporate career I was promoted into a role with an inspirational female boss Angela* who I admired greatly. She spearheaded the "Women in Leadership" programme, a mentoring scheme for high potential females in the male dominated technology company and held a top role on the senior team in Europe.

Excited to attend my first meeting with various business leaders alongside her, I was shocked at Angela's change in behaviour. It wasn't just smart flexing to attune to different people's perspectives, rather a Dr Jekyll and Mr Hyde scene. She had morphed into someone so unfamiliar, unrecognisable and incongruent that I was completely unhinged. It simply felt false.

At the end of the meeting she quipped "that's lesson number one Gill – just give them what they want to hear". I can still remember standing, rooted to the spot with my mouth wide open not able to speak as her heels clattered into the distance.

I learned so much in that role about the importance of being authentic. Showing up as the real you despite the job title or perceived expectation. And the importance of consistent, congruent role modelling. Angela had no idea what a gift she had brought me in that meeting.

In order to be positive, conscious role models to others we have to be self-aware, to know ourselves and be true to ourselves. Self-awareness is the greatest gift we can offer ourselves. It is the point from which we can make our best choices and be the choreographer of the dance of our own life.

We are surrounded in our digital economy by "influencers" and "experts" and magic formulas to help us build our "tribe". There seems to be so much FOMO (fear of missing out) and "comparisonitis" (comparing ourselves to others) that get in the way and blur the reality of our beautiful uniqueness.

Sure, I understand we can all learn the digital formulae to help spread our leadership message into the world, but I believe values matter. When you are congruent with your values there is no resistance.

You will experience ease and flow in your life and your work and without trying, you will role model consistent alignment to the world. The greatest success comes from being yourself. From being authentically you and showing up that way consistently and with integrity. You are the difference that makes the difference, so ground yourself in that. You are your own best reference site. Be proud of who you are, embrace your uniqueness and be the role model you want to follow.

As my Granny used to say to me, "Be yourself Gill, as everyone else is taken".

And if Granny was alive today, she would be helping me create a ripple effect with the pebbles of the role model I want to be.

* Real names have been changed

About Gill McKay

Gill McKay has been a professional business coach for more than 20 years. Gill works with coaches, trainers and HR professionals to amplify their results through using  neuroscience in their work. Her teaching helps them to increase their clients' self-awareness, their emotional engagement and awaken their brains to help them achieve deep transformation and change.

As co-founder of MyBrain International and the profiling instrument MIND, she provides tools and resources for the appliance of neuroscience. She is also author of the best-selling book "STUCK: Brain Smart Insights for Coaches" which shares her coaching stories and how clients can create change by understanding the brain science behind their challenges. She describes herself to be "all about helping people to step into the best version of themselves".

Gill lives in West London with her husband Moray, her three children, Gregor, Ellie, Georgina and her beloved chocolate Labradors, Gordon and Charlie. Contact Gill at www.mybrain.co.uk

REMEMBERING YOU ARE A STARSEED

By Rosanna Hanness

Ready to stop apologising for yourself?

You're not who you think you are anyway. It's time to get that desire fire burning SiStar...show the world just who you are.

It all looks 'good' on the surface, right?

But you probably wake up at night, between 3 and 5 a.m. wondering what else there is to life. How would it feel if you stopped being so darn busy keeping everyone else happy and just did YOU?

'Just WHO do you think you are?', asked the voice in your head again, the familiar pointy finger speaking.

'Let me SHOW you who I AM!' Said the little light inside, ready to shine brightly.

Firstly, you are not your personality. You learned your personality from your time in the womb, so that you could survive the world you were born into. Yup, you learned attention-seeking tactics of your Mum's and Dad's , from conception.

Anticipate the needs of others? Tick.

Put others before me? Tick.

Be 'nice', 'thoughtful', 'considerate'? Tick, tick, tick.

Get sick or injured when it's all too much? Tick.

Co-dependency? Tick.

But what does that actually mean? It means you will commit to staying small, to not rock the boat, to prevent people from feeling inadequate around you. Consider the marriage vows, 'to honour and obey'.

But you are not the roles you play.

Frustrated wife; never good enough mother; once upon a time lover; too busy friend; seething sister; worried daughter; I've got my shit together but secretly, anxious boss; hyper self-critical peer; well meaning, but resentful, volunteer.

You are not the opinions you've learned: to regurgitate. To sound interesting; well informed; educated but not too rebellious. The playground chat, the dinner party chat, the coffee break chat - all nicely influenced by everything around you, dressed up as you actually choosing what you tune into.

But choosing from what exactly? A pre-laid menu of more of the same, dressed prettily in different outfits.

You are not your body or your mind. You are not your past traumas and memories left behind. You are not the secret fantasies you dare never share. You are not the one apologising and pretending that you care.

Then, just who are you?

Now is your time to tell the world. Speak these words out loud and feel them in every fibre of your being...

I AM MultiDimensional.

I AM wild, audacious, raw and compassionate.

I AM all my shadow and my light

I AM so darn RAH! that if you saw me strip the BS away, you'd literally be blown away.

I have the mighty power to turn to that pointy finger and say, 'Want to know just WHO I AM? Move OUT of the way.'

I'll show you me, me stripped of my ego identity, all that struggle and 'lack' conditioning- all the self limiting beliefs and constant belittling.

I AM MY SOUL. I AM Infinite Love Light.

My body is ancient. It carries the cellular memory of my bloodline ancestors. But it is NOT me. It is a part of me, a transient suit to house my eternal BEINGness, whilst visiting this planet called Earth.

And what am I REALLY doing here?

I AM here to awaken passion within me and leave a legacy. I AM a droplet in the ocean of love, a unique Divine Spark – ready to awaken compassion within my own heart'.

This all sounds LOVELY. But just HOW do you translate this into your perceived 'reality' and the day to day, 7-11, autopilot setting?

It is simple. Everything around you is....YOU.

The good, the bad, the ugly.

And it's ALL random. Yup, random.

You're here, a droplet of consciousness in a random game of 'existence'.

The point of the game? EXPERIENCE.

So what DO YOU want to experience?

This is subjective and what you get to read, think and feel into and EXPLORE.

What DO YOU WANT to EXPERIENCE next?

Call it in.

You see, this game of life, it is all about asking questions rather than having the answers.

We are born egocentric, and we die egocentric - this means that as far as we are each concerned, the world DOES revolve around each of us. So does this universe.

If this is the case, what do YOU want to do with this knowledge and wisdom?

What changes do YOU want to see in me and in the world around YOU?

What is the most AUDACIOUS way YOU can go about co-creating this that is most enjoyable, graceful and easy? The most FUN expression of YOUR gifts?

These ARE the questions you want to ask yourself but don't expect answers! Allow confusion, not knowing, doubt, fear, anxiety and all that to surface. Let it all come out. That's all the BS that usually stops you from going any further into your self identity and enquiry.

Ask yourself, 'IF I wasn't scared, anxious, doubtful, uncertain of myself...WHAT would I do?'

HINT- usually, the stuff that really upsets you, that you get so caught up in and just CAN'T understand why nothing is done about it, that's a major clue as to what you have come here to contribute to.

BUT, and this is a HUGE but, your self sacrifice is NOT required.

Yes, read that again. Your self sacrifice is NOT required.

And by that I mean quit the martyrdom! STOP suffering for everyone else. NOW! Quit that shit!

It's unbecoming, unnecessary and down right counter productive. You are designed to thrive so get aligned with thriving, this is your duty.

HOW? Let's go back to this idea that you, that me, that we, are ALL. We are EVERYTHING.

Then your job is to master your own universe.

Make it what you want it to be, by resisting NO THING.

Yup, allow it, own it all. Especially what you find most difficult to swallow, accept, identify with.

The sooner you do this, the faster we all get liberated from our suffering, which is largely self-imposed.

Do I mean lie down and be a doormat?

Hell no!! AND heaven yes.

Translated: We need fear NO THING. NO THING has power over you, me or we.

Your soul transcends pain, death, poison, therefore, YOU ARE INVINCIBLE.

If you live from this space, then what?

Do you speak your truth? Do you call a lie a lie, even if it is YOU doing the lying (for you are everything)?

Tidying up our own inner world, landscape, back garden. What would happen if each of us did this?

I have a process that I live by. This helps me to have fun in my interaction with the world around me as I claim my Higher Self and sovereignty:

PUT YOUR SOUL IN CONTROL. Ego programming DOES NOT run your life anymore.

All you do is say, EVERY day, upon waking, peeing and brushing your teeth, 'I AM putting my soul in control. I AM surrendering to my Higher Self who already has what I want'

SET YOUR INTENTION. WHY do I want what I want? Check in with your soul and ego on every new thing you intend. Get clear on why you want it.

ALIGN ALL ASPECTS OF YOUR LIFE WITHIN YOUR CONSCIOUS CONTROL, WITH YOUR DESIRE. Even if this is only 10% of the power of you it's darned powerful to take inspired action.

SUBCONSCIOUS DETOX. Detox the parts of you that DON'T want what you consciously desire, those that WILL show up and say hello. Meet and greet them. Use the tools you have to embrace and entertain them. Up level if you need to, by employing those who have what you want, to show you HOW to cocreate it.

BLIND SPOT DISCOVER AND FINE TUNING. Where is your current consciousness at? What is showing up for you in your life, and ask if it either supports or seems to contradict what you desire. The process of aligning with the birth canal to your desires, takes refinement, discernment, and practice.

SELF MASTERY. You've nailed it. Now teach what you have mastered to those who wish to learn.

What if you used these steps to help you orientate through everything that seems too much to fathom…

Tricky relationship with your teen? Try it.

Lacking inspiration for the future of your business? Try it.

Need to spice up your love life? Try it.

Not sure whether to stay or go? Try it.

Look in the mirror every day, and decide who you want to be.

You chose to be here, today, in THIS body and THIS life. As amazing or as shitty as it feels, breathe it in.

Give yourself permission to rewrite the story of your life and then get on with LIVING the new one.

Your soul chose your earthly curriculum.

Why?

So you could remember that you are a StarSeed, reclaim your power and learn to co-create your soul desires.

Love up the past, raise the consciousness of humanity, reshape the future, by transmuting painful bloodline memories.

This is how we reunite with Source, ALL that is, all that was and ever will be.

About Rosanna Hanness

Rosanna is the Maverick behind the #StarPeace movement which seeds positive narrative into the collective consciousness of humanity through our media &  entertainment. As her soul frequency RozyGlow, she channels Divine Grace & delights in activating MultiDimensional Consciousness in Awakening StarSeeds- in particular those with a burning passion for world change who create the storylines we watch, read and listen to.

Her mission is to raise the frequency of the 'storytellers' who already have tremendous power and influence, so they create from their soul rather than ego wounding. This facilitates the balance of power shifting from external authority to internal sovereignty. Entertainment works directly with the subconscious of the collective, so is the fastest way to affect change quickly.

The creatrice of MultiDimensional Yoga and Coaching, Rosanna empowers those she works with to rewrite their narrative, raise their vibration and choosing to be part of the solution rather than the perceived problem. This is delivered through her 121 work with high profile creatives, her internationally acclaimed signature coaching program FearLESS, Loved Up & FREE 2 b ME and her public speaking Source Code transmissions. Rosanna is a Multidimensional success coach & Galactic healer who founded the StarPeace Movement. Contact Rozy at www.rozyglow.com

LEADING THROUGH A NEW TYPE OF CHANGE - MY HORMONAL CHANGES

By Adelle Helen Martin

"Be the change you want to see in our new world"

Adapted from Mahatma Gandhi

This is my personal story, sharing how I had to learn to lead through a new type of "change" due to the "clash of my change & career curves" – my menopause.

In response to "my clash" I created a new way for business women to lead themselves, their family, and career. There were no leadership books at the time of "my clash" and still none today, that would have ever prepared me for leading through menopause.

Yes, this is my personal leadership story, but more importantly, I have put pen to paper as I do not want business women going through what I did. Business women need knowledge and solutions to lead themselves and their family through their hormonal changes, and their career.

My Leadership Story – The Career *Curve*

151

My leadership journey started as a resilient 5-year-old girl. At the time I was called 'bossy' (it was the mid 70's) but as a gymnast and dancer I started to lead the younger children with their activities. At one event we were called back on stage and asked our names. That 'bossy' child froze and forgot her name (a little like menopause) and the audience erupted into laughter.

I was devastated and left the stage graciously with a speech impediment that would impact me for life. That resilient little girl did get back up and learn how to manage the impediment. It did not stop me building a rewarding leadership career spanning three decades in London.

Although, little did I know, that 35 years later I would leave the boardroom at the height of my career due to menopause. Why? Because one day I was in the boardroom presenting, but not only did I forget my name (like the 5-year-old on stage), I also forgot the topic I was presenting on!

The boardroom went very quiet, I made my excuses and left graciously with my speech impediment making an unwelcome return. Was my leadership career finished?

My Menopause Story - The Change Curve

Looking back now my hormone changes started when I was thirty-eight, we now know this as perimenopause. I had just accepted the "role of my career" two months ahead of the 2008 financial crisis. This turned out to be yet another opportunity for me to lead through an unexpected change using my resilience. To complement my new role, I started an MBA. My daughter was taking her GCSEs and being a mum was becoming less hands-on despite the odd lost netball kit that needed to be found on match days.

I should have been happy, but I wasn't. I could not even begin to understand why or share with anyone - including myself, why I felt so unhappy.

For the next two years I continued to lead my team through the financial crisis and my family through our own crisis. Nothing new, as I had done this with resilience for years and so it would work now - wouldn't it? But this time my resilience was not enough to get me through this change. This change was menopause, and nothing could have prepared me for the consequences of this new type of change.

The Clash of my Change and Career Curve

Remember the gracious exit from the boardroom? That night when I returned home, I took to my bed for three weeks completely broken. I was confused, my family and team were confused by what had happened to me. No one would ever have thought that "Ms Resilient" would ever get knocked down and stay down.

At the time I was misdiagnosed with chronic stress and exhaustion. Not happy with the diagnosis I pushed back explaining "it's more than stress, I'm so confused and broken". I have always been resilient, so why, this time when being knocked down, did I not get back up again?

Confused, lonely and exhausted by the experience, I took four months away from my career. I was desperate to understand what had happened to me. I wanted to be resilient again. I wanted to be there for my family and friends. I wanted to go back to my well-deserved career and lead my teams.

Working with my doctor and conducting my own research we finally pieced together what happened to me. To my complete shock I had gone through menopause. I looked at my doctor and said, "that's something my grandmother went through! I am only 40 and too busy for this!"

From my research and talking to business women I discovered that my menopause could have been accelerated due to high levels of stress. Some stress chosen and some circumstantial. On discussion with my doctor, they talked about "slowing down and considering an alternative career". So that was it! Aged 40 my menopause had impacted me, my family and career.

Being resilient, I was never going to make a choice after investing so much in both myself and my career. Yes, menopause knocked me down, but I wanted to "MenoGo" not "MenoPause" at 40.

I had to take ownership and learn how to lead through this new type of change. A change I knew nothing about and with little information from health care providers. But more interestingly, I found that women were reluctant to talk about it. With them saying "is it not better to say you had a breakdown rather than menopause!" I reflected and responded with a favourite quote "be the change you want to see in the world". Ironically this time saying "be the change" had a new connotation for me.

Taking Ownership and Being the Change

To be the change I wanted to see in the world I took ownership of my menopause and turned it into an opportunity. Using the four months away I embarked on research to:

Understand why my mind, body and relationships had changed so much

Establish how I could manage those changes

Find the medical truth about perimenopause, menopause and post menopause

Then, using the information, work out how to lead myself, family, and career.

As I progressed with my research, I realised that I had experienced a significant number of changes. There are 40 changes to manage! These impact our whole body and not just our ovaries, which came as a surprise to me. No wonder my change and career curves clashed! I was completely unprepared for the impact and consequences on my body, relationships, and career.

Through my research I quickly realised I was not alone. I spoke to women in workplaces and networking groups who were also impacted by their menopause. These business women had similar stories to me. I kept thinking, how many business women were trying to manage both their change and career curves? The data I poured over highlighted that:

● 90% of women say their perimenopause and menopause symptoms impact them

● 51% of women take time out of their business career due to their symptoms

- 32% of women leave their business or career as the impact of their symptoms becomes too much

With this revelation I just had to find a realistic solution that would help business women like me, lead in a new way to manage their menopause.

The Solution to Lead in My New World – The Menopause Resilience System™

When going through menopause as a business woman I wanted the solution to be easy to understand and implement. So, with the results of my research I grouped together my findings and solutions into four areas.

The result was my The Menopause Resilience System® to help businesswomen manage their menopause by teaching them to build a strong body. We need a strong body to lead in "our changing new world".

The Menopause Resilience System™ is one balanced system that focuses on our physical, mental, emotional, and spiritual wellbeing as we go through our hormonal changes. It contains twelve principles presented in four frameworks that teach us how to manage our changing body, mind, and relationships.

- Body | Feel Stronger

o Food: Eat to perform for optimal performance as our body changes

o Move: Movement to keep our changing body functioning and moving

o Snooze: Sleep to repair and rejuvenate as our body changes

- Mind | Think Clearly
o Calm: Managing our thoughts and keeping calm as our body changes

o Clarity: Keeping focused with our intention and energy

o Confidence: Building confidence so we can lead in a new way

- Relations | Manage Relationships

o Me: Self Leadership and the relationship with ourselves

o We: Group Leadership and the relationships with our family and friends

o Thee: Enterprise Leadership and the relationships with our workplace and networks

- Leadership | Take Ownership

o Vision: What is our True North - our purpose

o Mission: What will we do to go North - our outcome focussed goals

o Strategy: How will we go North - our own map with actions

Using my system, I was able to manage my menopause and lead myself in a new way. I built a strong body and felt stronger. I understood how my brain was changing so I could think clearly. I established how I was changing so I could manage the relationships with the people closest to me.

By feeling stronger, thinking clearly, and managing my relationships I was able to take ownership and lead myself through a new type of change I had never encountered before.

My new Career Curve

So, armed with my new approach to leadership, I headed back to my career and switched boardrooms, moving from Finance to Human Resources. I received amazing support from everyone on my return. I was given the opportunity to share my experience to help both women and men in the workplace.

As I spoke publicly, women reached out in support, sharing their personal stories and I was asked to co-lead the workplace Menopause Group. We provided a safe space where women came together to share stories, receive support, and influence workplace menopause policies.

I was starting to see the change in the menopause world, but I was restless. I knew there was even more I could do to support business women going through menopause. I wanted to approach Members of Parliament and work with menopause activists to highlight the lack of support for women going through menopause. My Mum says, "you are just like the suffragettes who fought for the right of women to vote - you are my "MenoGette".

So, approaching my 50th birthday "my present" was to coach businesswomen through The Menopause Resilience Club™ and raise awareness of menopause full time. A tough decision but one I do not regret.

My Summary

Yes, I found the consequences of not knowing what was happening to me isolating and frightening. I had not even heard of perimenopause and thought menopause was for older women and not me aged 40.

Sharing my story and creating The Menopause Resilience System® has helped many businesswomen to manage their menopause. I will keep the conversation going to empower women to take ownership and lead through this new type of change.

Leading Through a New Type of Change - Hormonal Changes

This should be an exciting era and a celebration, but so easily can become a challenge. Going through menopause will impact you, your relationships, and career or business. Menopause is talked about more than when I went through it. Yet still, menopause needs more support conversation medically, politically and in the workplace. So my advice for you:

·   Be curious and take the time to understand how your hormonal changes trigger your perimenopause, menopause and postmenopause.

·   Understand that it's not you! That it's not personal! It's how you respond to your changing body, mind and relationships that is important.

· Take ownership and think about how you can lead yourself, family and career or business through this new type of "change", a change you will have never encountered before.

And finally, "be the change you want to see in our new world".

About Adelle Martin

Adelle is an accredited Menopause Coach and Personal Trainer helping businesswomen to manage their menopause by teaching them to build a strong body using her own Menopause Resilience System™ so they can  continue to lead themselves, their family and business or career through their hormonal changes.

With a misdiagnosed early menopause as chronic stress, Adelle was forced to take time away from the boardroom and business. Adelle needed to understand what had happened and how she could manage her menopause!

Adelle did not want to choose between her menopause or business career. So, using her research Adelle developed The Menopause Resilience System™ to get herself "back to business".

Since getting "back to business" Adelle created The Menopause Resilience Club™ a private professional place to coach businesswomen to build a strong body to manage their menopause.

Adelle is also a Public Speaker, Menopause Activist sharing her personal story with the BBC, Host of The Business Woman's Menopause Show and Founder of The Women's Fearless Community Interest Company.

Email: adelle@executivemidlife.coach
https://executivemidlife.coach
https://twitter.com/coach_executive
https://linkedin.com/in/adelle-martin
https://www.facebook.com/executivemidlifecoach/
https://www.instagram.com/executive_midlife_coach/

EGOS, LIBERATED IMAGINATIONS, AND SMILES

By Gigi Brown

As a young Black, gay, female child growing up in a small, rural town in the United States in the early 1960s and 1970s, I remember feeling that I needed to suppress parts of myself. I did not feel that I could live openly as a Black, gay woman. I was aware that there were socially, politically, and religiously acceptable ways of being. During that period in my life, I was afraid that to go against societal norms might potentially place myself in emotional, mental, and even potential physical anguish. I did not consider the anguish that comes from showing up as less than one's true self. I also remember I was always both grateful and excited to read, hear, or see women courageously living inspired lives.

In retrospection, I would say I have always been interested in how people lead and what informs another's way of leading. As I, later in life, began the practice of meditation and surrendering to PRESENCE, how I lead changed.

Transforming away from oppression in the human experience – be it personal, institutional, interpersonal, or cultural - requires a collective shift from ego leading to spiritual consciousness leading. What am I saying? I'm saying that the intellect's (or the ego's) time of leading must now yield to the rise of a new consciousness. And this consciousness is one that honours the unique, diverse spiritual beings that we each are.

In the USA, where I live, it has taken 232 years from the forming of the Supreme Court for the confirmation of the first Black female justice to the Supreme Court, Justice Ketanji Brown Jackson, to occur. This lack of representation of women in visible, chief decision-making roles exists globally, in every country. And so, we really must ask ourselves what can we learn from women leading?

What can we learn from women leading?

We can glean much from women leaders who have turned their adversities into opportunities. I was in graduate school at Mercer University and had just finished my first class where we used the book, Let Your Life Speak: Listening for the Voice of Vocation by Parker J. Palmer. We were required to journal our thoughts weekly. Between the reading and the pages of my journal entries, I began to realise that I was seeking more than an advanced degree in Organisational Leadership. I was seeking to understand what it meant to lead from a place within myself, rather than from a place outside myself.

While conducting my research on women in the C-suite, specifically women CEOs, I discovered something vital regarding leadership. It is this: each of the three women I interviewed believed in herself. Each woman had no problem imagining herself in the leadership role she was in or had been in. In fact, each woman believed she had the ability to perform the requirements of the position and that she was deserving of the opportunity. They had high self-efficacy.

Their ability to keenly imagine and visualise themselves in the role of CEO was informed by a courageous trust in their inner wisdom. Their commitment and faith in their inner guidance system seemed to fuel their undertaking of roles they had not necessarily seen other women perform. I noted from the research that each participant acknowledged an inner desire to make something better and not just for themselves, but for others. It seems our internal desire to see better for others may move us beyond the ego's fear. What we can learn from women leading in unfamiliar territory is to have faith in our spiritual consciousness's ability to divinely guide our decisions and actions.

The Law of Spiritual Consciousness

First, what do I mean by spiritual consciousness? I am referring to the awareness of ideas, emotions, and thoughts that are beyond merely what we see before us and what we have intellectually learned. The Law of Spiritual Consciousness says once one becomes aware of a power within oneself that expresses ideas to prosper the individual and others, a connection to a vast, all-knowing consciousness of wisdom occurs. This omniscient power within us has always been with us. If we contemplate the existence of this power, we will find awareness of this creative power having nudged us throughout our life.

Some may prefer to think of spiritual consciousness as intuition – a gut feeling about people and situations, a knowingness. Whatever you choose to call this knowingness, women that lead despite their ego's limited knowledge, often lead from beyond the intellect's seen experiences. And they do so from this inner knowingness.

During my research studies at Mercer, I discovered that one of the characteristics associated with women leaders is the tendency to lead from the heart. Thus, women leaders are associated with leading more from a place within themselves than from purely the intellect. Interestingly, the study also revealed that these women, when selected for the role of CEO, are more likely selected to lead a company/organisation that is experiencing a crisis. Why? Because the women selected have often taken risks without the guidance from career experiences like their male counterparts.

The women are chosen because drastic change is needed to shift the trajectory of the crisis to one more favourable. To do this successfully, yes, the women use their intellect, but because they may not have the career or mentoring experiences to rely on, they must find within themselves something more sustaining. And this something is spiritual consciousness – awareness of an infinite source of divine ideas and solutions.

Why and how do women lead from spiritual consciousness?

Because women are under-represented in chief roles at companies, government, and religion, we have less visible examples of those that may look like us. Without a seat at the decision- making table, we must trust our spiritual consciousness.

If we want to see a difference in our lived experiences, we must imagine more for ourselves and more for others. And so, we look within ourselves for the strength, the imagination, the wisdom, the power, and the understanding to bring to light that which we have not seen before. It is from the influence of spiritual consciousness that we are inspired to move with zeal and love in renouncing the intellect's assessment of "this is too difficult; this is not possible at this time." Placed in unfamiliar territory in crucible times, we find stillness and are present to presence. We may inquire of an empty, silent room, "what now? What is the way forward?" And as we sit in quiet courage, we first feel a response – our intuition nudging us. Then the answer, the way forward beckons us. Then we gain the awareness that this knowingness has always been in us. It is always with us.

Women and anyone faced with crucible moments that require inner reflection and guidance, lean into spiritual consciousness because it is what shows up to help us when the ego has no clue. Less exposure to intellectually learned experiences opens the door to our intuitive guidance system. Thus, women in the workplace may be more open to welcoming spiritual consciousness at work. And for any one of us - when we are receptive to ideas and thoughts that are unsupported by intellectual experiences, we open the door to our divine imagination's ideas.

How does society prosper from women leading?

Women stepping into unfamiliar leadership roles with companies in crisis will face crucible moments and these crucible moments provide fertile ground for women to use their intuition, to call upon their omnipotent, omniscient spiritual consciousness. When we lead from a deep inner knowingness, we have the potential to inspire change from a different direction.

Women can help encourage the shift from ego led leadership to spiritual consciousness-led leadership. As we lead more from our spiritual consciousness, erroneous thinking and actions recede, and compassionate, diverse, equitable communities of wellbeing develop all over our vast, beautiful universe. When women lead, society prospers by recognizing and honouring diversity in perspectives.

Egos, Liberated Imaginations, and Smiles

The Global 500 lists 23 women CEOs, with six of these being women of colour. These numbers indicate progress. The numbers indicate lessening egos, liberated imaginations, and smiles of enlightenment. Our society prospers when any one of us from the seat of our soul vividly imagines and brings into the human experience, what our ego cannot yet see or imagine.

In 2019, whilst sitting quietly, listening to the voice of vocation, I heard clearly that it was time to resign from my managerial role. There was a different work for me to do and unlike the young me who was once afraid to be and follow the heart's call, I calmly and confidently wrote out my resignation. I remember a smile breaking gently and widely across my face that day.

What women and any person listening to spiritual consciousness offer is a lessened, liberated, smiling ego – glad to finally relinquish its control and to joyfully serve compassionately and lovingly as spiritual consciousness's ally for universal wellbeing.

About Rev. Gigi Brown

Rev. Gigi Brown is a truth writer, speaker, and ordained minister who is here as an intuitive messenger. She was ordained by Bishop Dr. Jack Bomar and studied under the late world spiritual leader Bishop Dr. Barbara King, and mentored by Rev. Dr. Sedrick Gardner.

She has published 'The Courage to Sit: Giving Forgiveness and Love to Yourself and Embracing a Life of Joy' and her next book due out in November is '49 Days: Taming the Ego'

Gigi holds immense gratitude and love for her ascended earth parents John and Goldia. Contact Gigi at www.gigibrownspeaks.com

ENDING THE 'BLAME-SHAME' GAME

By Jo Baldwin

Where does women's leadership need to go now?

It needs to go to a different place, a place that brings healing. It needs to start with forgiveness, a place that brings peace. It needs to end with compassion, a place that brings love.

After decades of fighting, struggling, striving; of uncovering discrimination, misogyny, patriarchy, abuse; of battling for equality, fairness, visibility; the time has come for the deepest change of all. To let go.

It is time to look deeper within, and delve into who we are in our essence as human beings and to find the potent elixir within us that can bring about equality.

The blame/shame game hasn't worked, it will never work, for anything but more of the same, for to project blame onto another is to see blame in ourselves.

Letting go and remembering who we are and how we were created, opens us a beautiful space to remember our true connection and creation, as one, masculine and feminine energy united.

Every single one of us is born divinely masculine and feminine within. Born as physically one or the other but in essence we exist in both worlds, in our internal energies, which offer a remarkable cocktail of creativity of service of joy.

Yet, over the last century, and for millennia, humanity has held itself in a place of division. For so long, it has been gender division, race division, ethnic division, poverty division, class division. All of which have been highlighted and fought bravely but my offering in this chapter is that we can stop fighting.

Let's change the record and stop looking outwards. Let's start with the I.

I have spent decades striving for equality, of tackling gender and sexual discrimination, in my own life and in society and organisations, but alongside my mission for many women I have uncovered and remembered who I really am.

I have dedicated and volunteered hundreds of hours holding meetings, handing out leaflets, standing my ground, attending hearings, as have so many others, perhaps, as have you have done, too.

Every minute was worthwhile and seeing women I have supported step into their first role in governance or management or entrepreneurship, has been a gift.

But recurringly I have felt a discord, and felt a deeper knowing that there is a better way, likely a more simple way. Now I can see what that is.

The power of we.

If we truly embraced ourselves as naturally and beautifully divinely male and female within we would remember that we are in fact one, as God/ the Universe/whatever your reference point is, made us. We are all souls, some of us very old souls. I have been a man and a woman. I have stolen, killed, hurt and deceived. I have loved, nursed, birthed and devoted my life to others. I offer that you have, too.

The point of life is to experience a journey of remembering. Not just in this life but in every life you have lived. I know I was with Yeshua, I was also with Adam, as part of my soul is Lilith. Who have you been?

Do you have recurring dreams of past times? Do you have unexplainable urges, talents or paranoias? Do you feel strongly connected to a certain part of history, a place, or a tribe?

I believe these are all signs of your soul's journey and what I call 'karmic nudges' that are reminding you of who you have been before.

Do you attract a certain type of person, situation, and feel like you are in a loop? Is there a pattern in your relationships or challenges that have come your way?

For me, I have nearly died many times, through illness, accident and another's hand. I have also attracted narcissist after narcissist, until I realised this and suddenly thought, why?

The Hawaiian process of Ho'oponopono is a true gift for all time. The elements create the opportunity to acknowledge, apologise, forgive and let go with love.

To blame anyone for anything, to hold on to bitterness and resentment with anyone, is to contain that energy within ourselves.

 As remarkable beings we are to be valued, with both creative and compassionate energy. If we allow ourselves to acknowledge, forgive, apologise, and let go we are looking at that bigger picture of the Universe and Multiverse.

By looking within and valuing our own balance of the masculine and feminine, we will reduce the need for pretending and abolish the desire to fit in. Where is 'in' anyway? 'In' does not exist. It refers to society but like so much of the English language, it refers to an old way where 'them and us' was the way, although really it wasn't. It never was.

By embracing yourself as a woman working in your own way, and bringing all of your divinity of who you are as a woman - thoughtfulness, compassion, kindness, consideration - to the board room of a male dominated table you will instantly change the outcome of the meeting. How? Because two things will be happening as you do this. Firstly those around the table will feel your congruence, your authenticity and your truth. They'll energetically feel it, and metaphorically 'smell' it. And secondly, this will open the floodgates for any men who may be there, too.

Casting my mind back now I shudder at how I behaved and the energy I took to the boardroom table of policing. I was hung up and obsessed with playing the role of a powerful, independent woman, in fact, a man. I tried hard, day in, day out, to be like the nine men in my group, and the exhaustion and depression it eventually caused, caught up with me. And I wasn't just exhausted from pretending, I was tired from hiding who I really was, and on a soul level this is the biggest disconnect of all.

As is in the Laws of the Universe and God, I naturally attracted the karmic energy which tested this 'pretend' me. Harassment, abuse and grief came to me both on the streets, and in the station. I had four attempts at my life, five internal hearings/enquiries and simply put, attracted lots of crap. My ego was happy being a victim and my inner child was happy blaming everyone else. I was emotionally confused and spiritually in turmoil, but all around me I saw other women managing their own challenge of existing in what can be, a very toxic environment.

In my final couple of years I became friends with a highly aspirational female officer who didn't stop surprising me. This woman, who is now one of the commissioners at the Metropolitan Police, was completely authentic in not only bringing her personality to work, but her femininity and her strength, too. She spear-headed many new policies and support groups. She was a role model that female policing desperately needed, and probably still does. As the Met seeks a new leader at the time of print I pray she takes the role, for as I experienced and observed that female officer being herself, being vulnerable, being compassionate and being fearless, I witnessed a different narrative and I suddenly felt hope.

It is time to let go of the anchor of inequality that's held us in a certain spot in the ocean of life. We can collectively forgive all that has come before, those who have been a part of what has come before, for by doing so, we in fact, forgive ourselves.

Being held, stagnant, in this place of division and blame has prevented us from reaching our true potential as a human race; as a united force of souls who have limitless potential to solve poverty and hunger and to create peace.

We could move on and sail towards a place of such joy, a place of such belonging, a place of valuing each other for all that we choose to be, if we do just one thing. We learn to let go.

Nature shows us in our own seas that we are here to evolve. That we can adapt very quickly to what we find ourselves in or the surroundings that we suddenly have.

Nature shows us that there is no rulebook, that both masculine and feminine can create and can offer different aspects of existence. It is simply within us.

We can start to really take responsibility, not control, but *responsibility*. And also to see the joy in and gratitude of being all that we are. Yes, the planet is a challenging one right now, but today is the first day of a new future and offers limitless potential.

Today, right now, by embracing the light and the potential of who you are wholly, fully, as both masculine and feminine energy, and by allowing yourself to express your heart and soul as your truth, you will begin to feel the peace we collectively seek.

Today by seeing the light within you, ready to shine in your own way, you will begin to see the light within others, whatever their gender, background or story.

Today by letting go of the narrative playing in your thoughts, and begin a new story of being present and expressing yourself fully, as divinely feminine and masculine, as simply you, you are united and equal.

It is no coincidence that there are many indigenous messages in this book. Since the first Women Leading book our human kind have dug deeper. It has been an honour to begin this book and end with the beautiful offerings from Hawaii. Our elders and the elders of theirs, have seen it all, and I feel it is time to remember that all of the answers we seek are in their eyes, their songs and their stories.

Love and blessings to you and to end I offer you the four steps of forgiveness and love in the form of Ho'oponopono:
Recall the experience or relationship which you wish to bring in the love and forgiveness to. Complete the following sentences and allow your voice of your heart to flow:
I am sorry I…
I forgive you…
Thank you for…
I love you

About Jo Baldwin

Jo is a powerfully intuitive and compassionate soul guide, mentor and healer. Her soul of Lilith has returned to heal the oldest wounds and to invoke forgiveness, especially to the divine masculine energy.

As an author Jo has published words on leadership, joy, health and energy. Most recently she has published 'Women Leading In Our New World' under her publishing house ProperBooks.

Jo's first coffee table book, VIBE a visual explosion of colour, and portal of positive energy, lifts lounges and spaces around the world. As the patron and trustee of charity Soul Sisters: Empowering People, Jo promotes awareness and encourages support for those who have experienced domestic violence, both men and women. She also volunteers writing workshops as part of the Safehaven Project for vulnerable men in Brighton

Based on the Sussex coast, UK with her two children she swears by yoga, likes to write songs and loves most to be on the beach watching the sunset in Hove or Santa Barbara. Contact Jo at www.jobaldwintrott.com

Made in United States
Orlando, FL
30 July 2022

20193742R00114